COLOR
GUIDE TO FLOWERING
PERENNIALS

COLOR

GUIDE TO FLOWERING

PERENNIALS

By Susin Leong & Tracy Loughlin

bay books

CONTENTS

Flowering perennials are more than just plants that grow and bloom for years and adorn our gardens. In the fickle world of flowers, perennials are the classics, the sentimental choices, the plants that find lasting places in our hearts, permeate our souls, and create meanings in our lives. From schoolyard daisies, to window-box pelargoniums, to a mother's favorite rose, these flowers have a familiarity that resonates deep within our gardening psyche.

With flowering perennials, gardeners can develop relationships as well as create garden designs. We nurture these plants season by season, awaiting the palpable moments when flowers open or leaves unfurl. We observe them over the years, and grow them for generations. Sometimes they stay with us all our lives, transplanted from home to home, and from garden to garden—becoming part of who we are as gardeners. Flowering perennials link the gardens of our past, present and futures.

Flowering perennials are the garden's sentimental favorites. They provide colorful highlights, season after season, and year after year.

By horticultural definition, perennials are plants that live for many years: technically, this is more than three, but, unlike trees and shrubs, perennials don't become woody with age. In gardens, perennials may be more broadly defined—they can include soft-stemmed or short-lived shrubs, as well as plants that are naturally perennial but grown as annuals or biennials depending on the garden's climate or design.

Generally, perennials are classified by their natural growing habits as herbaceous, evergreen or semi-evergreen. But, it's important to remember that these definitions can also be determined by the climate in which the plants are grown.

Evergreen perennials grow continuously throughout the year,. though they may slow down in certain seasons such as winter; and they don't lose all their leaves at once (if they do, they're usually in trouble). Evergreen perennials are the stalwarts of many garden designs because they have foliage all year round. And, in the case of some evergreens, the leaves are just as ornamental as the flowers.

Flowering perennials have a great variety of growth habits, foliage form, and flower; there is a range of plants for all climates and garden styles.

Semi-evergreen perennials are an intermediate group, with growing habits that fall between herbaceous and evergreen. These plants have a partial dormancy period, when their leaves and stems stop growing or they die back a bit but not completely. More than any other type of perennial, the behavior of semi-evergreens can depend on climate. For example, herbaceous perennials that originate in frost-affected cool climates may not become fully dormant during warm-garden winters; while tropical-natured evergreens can lose a few leaves if grown where winters are cold.

Herbaceous perennials have seasonally based lifecycles, growing and resting in a set pattern each year. They usually produce new leaves and grow rapidly in spring and summer, then flower in spring, summer or fall. After flowering, these plants tend to collapse in exhaustion—their growing cycle over for another year. The leaves and stems die off, and the plant goes to sleep. The dormancy of these perennials coincides with winter, ensuring the plants survive the shortened days, cold and frost; but depending on their origins, they may rest through other seasons instead: for example, some herbaceous perennials of Mediterranean or South African origin are dormant during the hot dry summers.

In the garden, and in pots, flowering perennials mix well with each other, but they can also be grown with shrubs, trees, foliage plants, and annuals.

In garden designs, flowering perennials are among the most varied and versatile of ornamental plants. Some are naturally associated with meadows and woodland gardens, or synonymous with cottage styles or flower borders. Others invoke their exotic origins in tropical jungle-like settings or sun-drenched rockeries with Mediterranean themes. And, of course, many of the flowering perennials will also thrive in pots.

From the tiniest ground cover to the loftiest field flower, there are flowering perennials in all shapes and sizes, for any climatic situation and any garden purpose. And, between them, there are flowers in every season and in colors of every dazzling hue.

When placing perennials in gardens, apart from considering their qualities of foliage and flower, always follow the basic rules of design. For example, the tallest plants should be at the back of borders or in the center of beds, with the lowest-growing ones at the front or around edges, and the medium-heights filling in between. Avoid solid blocks of a single color. Experimenting with the tones and playing with shapes and texture will add interest to any planting scheme. But remember that perennials aren't always the easiest plants to control—depending on the individual or its growing conditions—and this is part of their charm.

Perennials can create all kinds of garden themes, from carefully colored borders to free-ranging drifts. PREVIOUS PAGES: Yellow coneflowers and dahlias.

These days, many perennials are likely to be procured at the local garden center but they are also available through specialist nurseries. Before planting any perennial, it's worthwhile preparing the soil. These plants will (hopefully) be around for years, so give them a good start. Ideally, the soil should be enriched at least a few weeks before planting, with aged organic material (for example, well-rotted animal manure, humus-rich leaf mulch or your best compost). Turn this through the planting area, keep the soil moist, and watch for weeds. In containers, use quality potting mixes. If special conditions are required, such as acidic or alkaline soil, or added coarse material for drainage, also attend to these before planting.

Perennials that are purchased in containers, as they are from most garden centers, can simply be planted out. Loosen the roots just slightly, and trim off any dead or broken bits. In its new position, whether in the garden or in another pot, place the plant so that the soil is at the same level as it was in the original container.

Bare-rooted perennials are usually obtained from specialist nurseries and via mail-order catalogs. The plants are often field-grown and available during their dormant seasons (such as late fall and winter). Not only is it a joy every time they arrive—bunches of roots and divisions, labelled, packed in a box and full of promise—but buying bare-rooted perennials ensures you have access to the best range of plants and flowers.

Many flowering perennials are now grown and matured for sale in pots or in punnets. These can provide instantly satisfying results in garden designs.

Bare-rooted perennials need to be planted immediately in the garden, and preferably in soil that is prepared in advance of their arrival. Make sure the hole is twice as large as the root spread, trim any broken or overly long roots, and carefully place the plant in position. Fill in with rich, friable soil, packing it firmly around the roots; but keep the crown of the plant above soil level and uncovered. If a delivery of these perennials is badly timed and catches you unprepared, the plants can be temporarily accommodated in a nursery-style bed, in a sheltered part of garden.

Always give newly planted perennials a gentle but thorough soaking to help them recover. A very dilute seaweed-style preparation after planting may also help to stimulate the growth of new roots. Mulch around the base of new perennials, too, but do not let any of these materials touch the stems or suffocate the crowns.

Regular watering will help new perennials to get established, especially if they are being planted during warm seasons. Bare-rooted plants, in particular, will need careful attention to watering to ensure that they don't dry out while trying to re-grow.

Always give your flowering perennial plants a good start in the garden. FOLLOWING PAGES: Once established, these plants will reward for many years.

Once they are settled in appropriate garden conditions, many flowering perennials will simply live by the seasons, year after year, and require almost no maintenance. Most will thrive and flower better if they are watered deeply and regularly during the growing seasons (for example, once a week in spring and summer, depending on the plants and the conditions); however, some are also naturally tolerant of drought.

Fertilizing is also uncomplicated, especially if perennials are planted in well-prepared, enriched soil and an organic mulch is used throughout the year. A light sprinkle of slow-release fertilizer, preferably one for flowering plants, or a top-dressing of compost can provide a seasonal boost in spring and summer. There are also many pre-mixed formulations that are easy to use for those, like roses or orchids, with special needs.

Depending on the plant's habits, judicious pruning may also enhance results. The evergreens or ground covers rarely need more than a trim and tidy to shape them or keep them dense. With herbaceous types, the foliage is simply cut back to ground level once it naturally dies down. Semi-evergreens may be pruned back by about half in winter to encourage new growth in spring. But, for many flowering perennials, the removal of finished blooms, also known as "deadheading," is the only pruning they need: this extends their flowering seasons, by encouraging new buds to be produced, and also helps to keep plants shapely and compact in growth.

For some of these flowering perennials, removing finished flowers (or cutting flowering stems for the vase) is all the routine maintenance they need.

As a group, flowering perennials are generous plants. They bloom freely and grow easily, but they multiply rapidly too—which means that you can quickly fill your garden and realise your design inspirations.

Like all flowering plants, these perennials set seed; and, with species, new plants can be produced in this way. But note that variations can occasionally occur in seedlings (though these can be fun, or even become famous), and some species can take many years to reach flowering size. Also, many cultivars and hybrids are unsuitable for seed collection because they may not produce seed, or their seed may be infertile, or their seedlings may revert to a natural form without the parents' selected traits.

The majority of flowering perennials also reproduce by other means, a tactic that naturally enhances their chances of survival. These perennials may trail, with each wandering stem sending down roots from which new plants develop; or they can grow from rhizomes or tubers that multiply underground; or form clumps with offshoots that eventually replace the original plant. They are easily propagated by cuttings, divisions of clumps or root divisions, and new plants produced in these ways will be identical to the parent and are relatively quick to mature and flower.

Among the perennials are some of the most popular plants in cultivation, such as the pelargonium—a favorite among gardeners for centuries.

In this book, we have chosen to present flowering perennials in their color groups—hot, warm, cool, pastel and neutral—because color is a defining factor in garden design, and one of the flower's most memorable characteristics. Of course, none of these plants are limited by the chapter in which they appear, and many flowering perennials include a wide color range among their species, varieties and cultivars. We've also included plants that aren't "perennial" according to horticultural definitions, but in gardens they are commonly grown as such. And because roses, irises, and lavender occupy special places in gardeners' hearts, we have honored them separately here.

The selection of plants is by no means definitive—in books as in gardens, some flowering perennials we simply could not fit in, love them as much as we do. Instead, this title has been composed as a collection of favorites, and is intended as an introduction, a guide.

Welcome to the infinitely colorful world of flowering perennials—we hope you plant, and enjoy.

Hot colors bring the garden to life. They are energetic and raise our heartbeats. Hot-colored flowers aren't blooms that sit sedately in quiet corners—they want to be noticed. In the garden, hot colors are much better when celebrated with abandon. Never hold back. They look best when splashed about with imagination, in wild and carefree combinations.

Hot colors evoke the exotic nature of gardens. This tropical design features brightly toned foliage plants, such as bromeliads, as well as a host of hot-colored flowers. PREVIOUS PAGES: *Paeonia lactiflora* hybrid.

Red is hot. On the color wheel, all the hot colors have a good dose of red, but also varying degrees of yellow or blue. In the garden, apart from appearing in flowers, hot colors are evident in more subtle forms, in bud, fruit, bark, stem, and leaf. Naturally, hot flowers always stand out because the opposite color to red is green, but they can also be contrasted with lighter tones.

Hot-colored flowers are best celebrated in carefree combinations that take advantage of their bold natures. RIGHT: Various cultivars of *Lampranthus*.

In this chapter we have gathered together flowering perennials in hot colors, from shocking magenta to cinnabar to pure red. Of course, many perennials in general can have flowers in hot tones, depending on the species or cultivar, and some of these have been included in other chapters. Hot-colored schemes can also be blended with warm tones, or highlighted by pastels.

Hot-colored flowers are naturally contrasted by green foliage but they will also blend with other colors. FOLLOWING PAGES: Hot colors create the most dramatic and exciting of garden designs.

ASTER SPECIES & CULTIVARS

ASTER

Perennial asters flower
from late summer and
throughout fall,
depending on the
species or cultivar.

Perennial asters are commonly known as the Michaelmas daisy in northern hemisphere gardens and as the Easter daisy in southern parts of the globe, because they may flower at the time of these religious occasions. Asters form an enormous group within the flowering world's greatest family— Compositae or Asteraceae, the daisies. Among the most familiar of these perennial asters are the herbaceous species *Aster novae-angliae* and *A. novi-belgii*, both of which originate from North America, along with all their many derivatives.

Perennial asters are mostly grown for their brightest of jewel-bright flower heads—from brilliant red and magenta to electric purple and blue, as well as softer pink, lilac, and white— contrasted with a gleaming yellow center. Although the plants are naturally compact in shape, they are very fast-growing,

even in a single season. There are also dwarf forms that are ideal for small-scale garden designs or containers.

GROWING NOTES

Perennial asters prefer cool to warm climates, full sun, and well-drained soil. Light shade is tolerated but the plants won't be compact in growth or prolific in bloom, and their flower colors will be diluted and less than dazzling. In the right conditions, and watered regularly and generously during spring and summer, the plants can grow quickly into large clumps. Cut finished flower stems close to ground level, to prolong the flowering season. Established clumps may be divided while plants are dormant in winter.

Perennial aster flowers are long-lasting when cut for arrangements, and removing stems also prolongs the plant's flowering season.

AUBRIETA DELTOIDEA
AUBRIETA

In spring, the flowers of aubrieta almost cover the plant's dense mat of minute leaves.

This tiny perennial billows along with diminutive leaves forming a dense cushiony mat, then bursts brightly into flower in spring. Aubrietas grow only to 6 in (15 cm) in height, and their gray-green foliage and trailing ground-covering habits naturally suit edgings, stone walls, steep banks, and rockeries, as well as exposed garden areas and coastal conditions. Cultivars of *Aubrieta deltoidea* can have crimson, magenta, pink, lilac, or violet flowers; and there are also forms with semi-double flowers or variegated leaves.

GROWING NOTES
Aubrietas will grow in most garden climates except tropical or very arid areas, and they are also tolerant of frost. The plants particularly like full sun and fast-draining conditions. Light, sandy soils are also preferred. Do not overwater, especially during fall and winter. After flowering is finished, cut back plants to shape them or to keep them compact. Propagate the cultivars by cuttings only.

AECHMEA, BILLBERGIA & OTHERS
BROMELIADS

One of the wonders of the botanical world, the bromeliad family, Bromeliaceae, is large and diverse, with plants of various growth habits and habitats. These include epiphytes (plants that live "above ground," for example hanging on trees or on rock cliffs) and terrestrials (plants that live on the ground). Ornamentally, there are many bromeliads commonly grown, including *Aechmea, Billbergia, Guzmania, Neoregelia,* and *Tillandsia.* For commercial harvest, however, there is only one: *Ananas comosus,* the pineapple, "discovered" by Christopher Columbus in the West Indies.

In garden settings, bromeliads define tropical styles and rainforest themes but these plants are also effective in modern designs. They are adaptable, too. With near-succulent strap leaves, often themselves strikingly colored or striped, and surreally shaped flowers of fantastic hues, lasting many weeks, sometimes months, the bromeliad becomes a self-contained display that requires almost no effort to maintain.

Bromeliads are surreal, but many species, such as *Aechmea* (above) and *Neoregelia* (right), are also easy to grow.

Many bromeliads will thrive indoors, creating a long-lasting display of sculptural flowers and leaves.

GROWING NOTES

Most bromeliads originate from the tropical or subtropical jungles of the Americas. Many, like *Aechmea*, are epiphytic—anchored by their roots to high or hostile places—and have a funnel-like formation of leaves that traps water and other nutrients in the plant's center. Others, such as Spanish moss, *Tillandsia usneoides*, have barely any roots and simply drape themselves over their hosts. Some, such as the pineapple, are purely terrestrial.

Most bromeliads thrive in warm and moist environments, but some tolerate cool conditions with protection from frost. Many will grow indoors. In containers or garden beds, they require a very coarse medium, such as the chunks of bark used for orchids. Epiphytic plants need high humidity and appreciate regular misting, especially in hot, dry weather.

CENTRANTHUS RUBER

RED VALERIAN

With very little effort, red valerian grows without bounds through the garden, creating a sweep of color as it goes. It is vigorous and evergreen, with thick lance-shaped leaves and a dense habit crowned by tightly packed panicles of red or pink star-shaped flowers from spring throughout summer to fall. Only one species, *Centranthus ruber*, is cultivated but there is also a white-flowering form. The flowers of the species readily set seed and wild seedlings can appear almost anywhere—vacant patches of garden bed, gaps in paving, rockery pockets—establishing themselves with ease.

Grown in a drift, red valerian creates a sweep of color from spring throughout summer to fall.

GROWING NOTES

Red valerian thrives in almost any climate except the tropics, especially if given full sun all day and very well drained soil. The plants are extremely tough and can withstand harsh growing conditions including drought, malnourished soil, large rockeries, and steep slopes. Remove flower heads before they produce seeds to prevent self-sowing (unwanted plants are easy to pull out), and to prolong the season of blooms.

CISTUS SPECIES & HYBRIDS
ROCK ROSE

The fragile beauty of its flowers belies the hardiness of the rock rose. These evergreen plants from the Mediterranean region are tolerant of coastal conditions, strong winds, poor soils, frost, and drought. They live long but flower young, and profusely. The genus, *Cistus*, includes rangy and unstructured shrubs, and more compact perennial-type hybrids. Their leaves are aromatic, lance-shaped, and dark green, a perfect foil for the spectacular spring and summer blooms with papery petals in lilac, pink, white, or magenta.

GROWING NOTES
Rock roses prefer a climate with hot dry summers and cool wet winters, similar to their Mediterranean origins, and full sun and well-drained soil. They struggle in areas with high summer rainfall or humidity, or in heavy or waterlogged soils. Tip-pruning of young plants helps to keep their habits dense and tidy; older plants should be cut back after flowering. Once established, plants rarely need regular watering.

The rock rose has a vigorous shrub-like habit: many of the hybrids, such as *Cistus* x *purpurea* (right), have larger flowers than the species.

CYCLAMEN SPECIES
CYCLAMEN

For more than 500 years cyclamens have been in cultivation but it was the trend-setting florists of 19th-century Europe who turned these tuberous perennials into flowering superstars. Although they originate from a limited area, only around the Mediterranean Sea and southern Europe, cyclamens are admired and grown all over the world. The florists' cyclamen, *Cyclamen persicum* and derivatives, is usually potted for short-term indoor decoration. In the garden, the Neapolitan or ivy-leaved cyclamen, *C. hederifolium*, is often preferred: its marbled foliage forms a dainty clump and the plant produces a long succession of red, pink, or white flowers throughout the fall.

Upward-sweeping petals characterize the cyclamen's flowers. Some, like the florists' cyclamen, have fancy frilled blooms.

GROWING NOTES

Perennial garden cyclamens, such as *C. hederifolium*, can be grown in warm to cool climates. These prefer woodland conditions, such as under deciduous trees, where they receive sun in winter but are in dappled shade for the warmer months. The plants also enjoy well-drained soil that is rich in organic matter, but the tubers must be kept dry while dormant.

DAHLIA SPECIES & CULTIVARS
DAHLIA

The dahlia is an inspirational flower: whole gardens are devoted to it, societies form in its worship, shows are held to honor it, some plant breeders have given their lifetimes in pursuit of its perfection, and even the rich and famous have been wooed (the Empress Josephine, wife of Napoleon Bonaparte, was an early and influential fan). Everyday gardeners, too, have embraced the dahlia and made it a sentimental favorite of cottage gardens, potagers, and borders. And florists and designers, of course, are ever-excited by the infinite potential of its flower color and form.

Horticulturally, the dahlia has come a long way. From a handful of humble ancestors originating in the mountains of Mexico and South America, these plants have fast evolved, through hybridization, into a dynasty of groups based on flower forms—including single, anemone, pompom, peony-flowered, cactus-flowered, decorative, waterlily, and collarette. Fortunately, most gardeners need not be overly concerned with

For centuries, dahlias have appealed to gardeners and other flower-lovers: public demand and private devotion have resulted in a vast array of flower colors, sizes and forms.

official groups or standards—with such a vast array of dahlias easily accessible, we can simply choose the flowers we like on plants that suit our climates.

GROWING NOTES

Dahlias can be grown in most gardens except tropical. They do especially well in conditions that resemble their ancestral cool moist mountain habitats. The plants grow from a tuber, producing lush foliage in spring followed by flowers throughout summer and fall. All growth dies down as the weather cools, and the plants become dormant for winter. Depending on garden conditions, the tubers can be lifted and stored or left in the ground. The tubers, once lifted, may be divided, and dahlias can also be propagated by cuttings. For gardeners who become enthused, it is worth seeking out specialist dahlia growers and societies.

Dahlias are officially classified by their flower types and there are many hundreds of cultivars available. Most will bloom in summer and fall.

DICENTRA SPECTABILIS
BLEEDING HEART

This ornamental gem of the cool-climate garden is as delicate as its common name suggests. A herbaceous perennial originating from Japan, *Dicentra spectabilis* has twin-spurred flowers like little pink and white caricatures of hearts. The plant has deeply divided leaves, giving it a fern-like appearance, and grows throughout the warmer seasons into a clump about 2 ft (60 cm) in size before the leaves fall and it lies dormant for winter. The pendent flowers on long curved racemes are produced from mid to late spring, for several weeks of wonder. There is also a white-flowered cultivar, 'Alba.'

GROWING NOTES
The bleeding heart thrives only in moist and cool positions, such as in the filtered shade of trees. It resents hot sun and harsh wind, and will appreciate a deep friable soil that is rich in organic matter. Remove flower stems as they finish, and cut foliage to the ground after it yellows and dies down. Established clumps may be divided when the plant is dormant.

Dicentra are best in cool, woodland settings. The twin-spurred flowers, like little hearts, hang from arching racemes.

DIERAMA PULCHERRIMUM
FAIRY FISHING RODS

With flowers like fluted bells swaying from gossamer-fine pedicels, all hanging along an arching wand, fairy fishing rods transform the garden into a place of enchantment. Native to South Africa, this cormous perennial is not the easiest to obtain, but the magical effect is well worth any effort. *Dierama pulcherrimum* has fine, reed-like evergreen leaves that form a dense clump and complement the delicate stems of flower which are silvery-pink in the species, but also pure white or dark pink in cultivars. In gardens, watery settings, such as beside a pond, enhance the reed-like beauty of its leaves and the fairyism of its flowers.

GROWING NOTES
Dierama prefers cool climates but will adapt to warmer regions. The plants require full sun all day, and a well-drained soil that retains moisture in spring and summer (when they should be generously watered). Clumps are formed when the corms produce offsets; these may be divided but are very slow to re-establish and flower.

The fluted bell flowers of fairy fishing rods transform the garden into a place of enchantment.

ECHINACEA PURPUREA

PURPLE CONEFLOWER

Remedial qualities aside, the purple coneflower is a botanical marvel. Each flower head begins life as a tight bud of lime-green that daintily blushes pink; then opens, a giant of a daisy, with shocking pink ray petals around a contrasting brown center. As the flower ages, the central cone grows in size, becoming tinged with flaming orange; the ray petals relax downward, fading reluctantly but refusing to fall. If left to its own devices, the coneflower finishes its season dramatically, transformed into a hard dark urchin of seeds.

Echinacea flowers are produced from spring throughout summer into fall, with each bloom lasting for weeks.

GROWING NOTES

This herbaceous perennial grows in basal clumps of large leaves. It will thrive in many climates from warm to cold, except the tropics. The plants prefer full sun, but will tolerate slight shade. They like a well-drained soil though aren't fussy about its richness, and will also grow in pots. The species has pink or magenta flower heads, but there is also a white-petalled cultivar (see page 394). Cut flower stems are very long-lasting in arrangements.

FUCHSIA SPECIES & CULTIVARS

FUCHSIA

There are many fuchsia hybrids and cultivars available to gardeners, most flowering from summer to fall.

For 300 years, fuchsias have fascinated gardeners with their uniquely formed flowers—typified by an elongated calyx, four recurved sepals, four fluted petals, and prominent stamens, all in a pendulous arrangement. However, while there are many species in the genus *Fuchsia*, mostly native to tropical rainforests of central and South America, with a few endemic to New Zealand and Tahiti, only a handful of these have contributed to the vast array of hybrids: including *Fuchsia fulgens*, with long, narrow red flowers, and the red-and-purple-flowered *F. magellanica*.

The many thousands of hybrids available are testament to the fuchsia's popularity. Depending on the cultivar and the garden's climate, the hybrid fuchsias may be evergreen and shrub-like or prostrate, or woody-based herbaceous perennials that are

dormant during cold winters. The plants are classified by flower type—single, semi-double, and double—and the colors available range from white and cream through all the pinks and reds to dark purple and almost lilac-blue. Some flowers also have contrasting sepals and petals or gradual shadings of color.

GROWING NOTES

While the growing habits of hybrid fuchsias will vary according to the climate, most adapt to a wide range of conditions from cool to subtropical. Some plants are herbaceous and frost hardy, while others are tender and need to spend cold winters indoors or in sheltered environments. In warm, humid conditions, fuchsias may be subject to fungal diseases like black spot and rust.

For both garden-grown fuchsias and those in containers such as hanging baskets, tip pruning will encourage more compact growth and more flowers. Older, straggly plants may be pruned hard at the end of winter. All fuchsias are easily propagated from cuttings throughout the growing season.

Though tropical in origin, fuchsias are very adaptable to garden cultivation. Some types are frost hardy or herbaceous; others can be grown indoors.

GERBERA JAMESONII
GERBERA

In the past, the homegrown gerbera has been somewhat overshadowed by floristry's flamboyant varieties with their larger-than-life flower heads and unnaturally long stems. But the vast commercial efforts in hybridization driven by floristry have started to benefit gardeners, too, especially with the rise of potted color, and the range of gerberas for general cultivation is now more spectacular than ever. Where once only the orange-red flowers of the evergreen perennial species *Gerbera jamesonii* were common in gardens, modern cultivars now offer many colors including crimson, magenta, salmon pink, apricot, and yellow. The flower heads are larger, too, and may have double rows of ray florets.

The natural flowering time for garden-grown gerberas is from spring to fall; removing the finished flower stems encourages more blooms.

GROWING NOTES

Gerberas prefer frost-free warm or tropical garden climates but can also be grown in pots indoors. Outside, they need full sun all day; for indoor plants, a brightly lit and airy position is best. The plants require well-drained soil and regular watering in spring and summer, with drier conditions in the cooler months. In pots or the garden, keep the crown of the plant above soil level.

GEUM CULTIVARS
AVENS

Whether intensely yellow, blazing orange, or drop-dead red, the flowers of *Geum* are outstanding. With their free-fluttering petals and prominent stamens, typical of the rose family to which they belong, these perennials have long been star attractions of the flower garden—particularly the double-flowered cultivars 'Mrs Bradshaw,' with rich scarlet flowers, and 'Lady Stratheden,' a pure bright yellow. Other types of avens are less easy to obtain but well worth the effort, including the striking tangerine-flowered *Geum* x *borisii*; the water avens, *G. rivale*, with nodding flowers; the rich apricot-colored cultivar 'Dawn'; and the pale lemon 'Moonlight.'

GROWING NOTES
Avens prefer full sun conditions in cool, moist climates. However, they will also adapt to warmer regions, especially if given some shade. The plants will tolerate frost but their usually evergreen habits may turn herbaceous. The large, lobed, hairy leaves of *Geum* grow in basal clumps, and, once established, these clumps may be divided to propagate.

Avens bloom from late spring to early fall, especially if finished flower stems are removed. 'Mrs Bradshaw,' with double red flowers, remains one of the most popular cultivars.

HELIANTHEMUM NUMMULARIUM
SUN ROSE

The sun rose well reflects its celestial name—the plant will thrive only in the brightest of garden conditions, its flowering season occurs around the solar peak of midsummer, and if light levels are too low the flowers will close in protest. Evergreen with low, spreading shrub-like habits, these plants are closely related to *Cistus* (see page 52), and the whole family often shares the common name of rock rose. New flower colors of sun rose continue to develop and now range from white to pale yellow and pink to orange and crimson, as well as a cultivar 'Raspberry Ripple', with bicolored flowers.

The blooms of *Helianthemum* will open only in the sun; many cultivars exist, with flower colors from crimson and pink to white.

GROWING NOTES

Helianthemum nummularium prefers cool to cold climates and regions of low humidity. The plants require full sun all day and very well drained, slightly alkaline soil. They are especially suitable for low borders, raised beds, rockeries, and other stone gardens; in the right conditions, these plants may live for many years. Trim plants after flowering, or in late winter, to keep them tidy and compact.

HETEROCENTRON ELEGANS
SPANISH SHAWL

This evergreen perennial provides great cover at ground level, growing into a low but dense carpet of interwoven red-brown stems and small, shiny, bright green leaves. In spring, the reason for its common name, Spanish shawl, is apparent as the plants become cloaked in brilliant cerise flowers (although the species, *Heterocentron elegans*, is actually native to Mexico and central America). In the right conditions, the plants will form a dense ground cover quickly and then live for many years. They are also suitable for pots and especially effective in hanging baskets and other containers which allow them to cascade.

Spanish shawl grows into a dense evergreen carpet and provides brilliantly bright flower color at ground level.

GROWING NOTES

These plants prefer warm and tropical climates, being intolerant of frost. They require partly shaded conditions, such as dappled light under trees or situations where they are protected from strong afternoon sun. Water well in warm seasons. Plants may be divided, or cuttings taken, in late spring and summer.

IXORA SPECIES & CULTIVARS

IXORA

The fiery-hued flower heads of ixoras have given the plants such names as jungle geranium, jungle flame, and flame of the woods. And although *Ixora* is a genus of about 400 species of tropical plants, only two are commonly cultivated. *Ixora chinensis* has large glossy evergreen leaves and can grow into a dense tall shrub in its natural state, but in gardens it is much smaller and is often seen as a potted specimen or indoors. The flowers of the species are red, but the most popular cultivar 'Prince of Orange' has clusters with yellow, orange, and scarlet blooms. *I. coccinea* has similar growing habits, and its cultivars have softer-colored orange-pink flowers.

The flowers of *Ixora chinensis* 'Prince of Orange' display many hues in each cluster; this cultivar flowers in summer and fall, and is often grown in pots.

GROWING NOTES

Ixoras need sheltered, warm, or tropical garden conditions; however, plants can also be grown indoors. They prefer dappled shade all day, or direct morning sun only, and well-drained soil that is organically rich. Lightly trim after flowering to keep the plants compact; if necessary, older plants may be pruned (cut back by about one-third) in late winter to rejuvenate them.

KALANCHOE BLOSSFELDIANA
FLAMING KATY

In the garden, the natural flowering time of *Kalanchoe blossfeldiana* is late winter to spring, but potted plants in bloom are available year round.

Possibly the best-known species of a large genus of succulent-leaved plants, *Kalanchoe blossfeldiana* originates from Madagascar, but its adaptability and appeal have ensured that it is cultivated all over the world. Flaming Katy, like many succulents, is very easy to grow in any frost-free climate and is also successful as an indoor plant. It is often sold as potted color and in full flower, with the plants covered in clusters of waxy star-shaped blooms.

The wild form of this species has red flowers, but hybridization has produced a greater variety of colors including deep crimson nearing purple, magenta, and pink and, more recently, yellow, orange, and almost white. There are also many other species and cultivars of *Kalanchoe* which are both colorful in flower and easy to grow—but none are as famous as flaming Katy.

Many *Kalanchoe* species and cultivars, such as *K.* 'Freedom Bells' (above) and *K.* 'Pixie Bells' (left), are easy to grow in gardens and also pots.

GROWING NOTES

Kalanchoe blossfeldiana thrives in a wide range of climatic conditions, from tropical to cool, but it does not tolerate frost or low winter temperatures. In the garden, the plants prefer morning sun only or filtered shade all day; indoors, they need bright light to flower. Whether in pots or the garden, a well-drained soil is essential—one of the few problems these plants encounter is waterlogging.

An evergreen, creeping perennial, its stems readily sprout roots wherever they touch the ground, allowing the plant to spread (hence cuttings are also very easy to strike). This sprawling habit, and its tough constitution, make the plant ideal for ground cover, especially in dry areas, or for hanging containers and other raised situations. Apart from trimming the finished flower heads to keep plants tidy and compact, they require almost no maintenance.

LAMPRANTHUS SPECIES
ICE PLANT

Burning bright as the sun under which they love to bask, the flowers of *Lampranthus* aren't just colorful, they actually sparkle. Purple, red, orange, yellow, pink, or cream—depending on the species or cultivar—the flowers cover the foliage completely and when the plants are massed, the effect is dazzling. Originating from South Africa, this large group of succulents includes many low-growing trailing or creeping perennial forms, such as *Lampranthus aureus*, *L. roseus*, and *L. spectabilis*, that make great ground covers. These can be used to stabilize soil, even sand, and they also tolerate low rainfall and no maintenance.

Sparkling bright, ice plants may flower in late winter or spring, depending on the species or cultivar.

GROWING NOTES

Ice plants easily adapt to a wide range of warm, frost-free climates, but they do require full sun (the flowers won't open without it) and well-drained, light soil. Water regularly only to establish plants and during prolonged dry periods in summer, and avoid fertilizing: the plants flower better in tough conditions. Species can be grown by seed, but *Lampranthus* is more easily propagated by cuttings.

LANTANA SPECIES & CULTIVARS

LANTANA

The cultivated lantanas have had to distance themselves from the wild members of their family, mostly due to the noxious reputation in many parts of the world of *Lantana camara*, a vigorous shrub with pretty cream-and-lilac flowers. Its modern cultivars, however, are dwarfed forms and sterile— purely ornamental—with improved and highly desirable flower colors of intense yellow, orange, pink, red, and mauve. Another affable lantana, *L. montevidensis*, is a trailing perennial that grows in tumbling thick cascades of fine leaf and profuse lilac flowers. This species is not invasive and is well suited to trailing situations, whether contained in a hanging basket or as expansive ground cover.

GROWING NOTES

Ornamental lantanas are very adaptable to most garden climates, and they will withstand light frost and also drought. The plants thrive most vigorously in warm conditions, where they may flower almost all year round. Trim lantanas to shape if desired, otherwise they require almost no maintenance.

The modern lantanas include multi-colored clusters of intense yellow to scarlet. The trailing, easy-growing species *Lantana montevidensis* (above) has profuse lilac-purple flowers.

LOBELIA CARDINALIS
CARDINAL FLOWER

The scarlet flowers of *Lobelia cardinalis* are borne on tall stems throughout summer; this perennial species loves a waterside setting.

The cardinal flower is one of the lesser-known lobelias in a genus full of flashy annuals. Unlike the short-lived but cheerful edging lobelias with blue and purple blooms (*Lobelia erinus* and its many cultivars), this herbaceous perennial grows to a stately height, up to 3 ft (1 m), and has tall upright stems of exclusively red flowers. *L. cardinalis* from North America is a known water-lover, thriving in marginal areas such as by streams and lakes or in marshy meadows. The species has also contributed to perennial hybrids including 'Queen Victoria,' which has dark burgundy leaves and stems and crimson flowers, and 'Russian Princess,' which has purple-tinged foliage and cerise-red blooms.

GROWING NOTES

Lobelia cardinalis prefers cool climates, full sun, and heavily enriched soils. However, it can also be grown in warmer areas if shaded from strong sun and watered generously in hot weather. Whether they are grown in watery aspects or in the flower garden, do not allow these plants to dry out in spring and summer.

LYCHNIS SPECIES
CAMPION

The vibrant, jewel flower colors of perennial campions are clearly enhanced by the plants' evergreen leaves— providing a simple but naturally outstanding contrast. Red is the predominant hue—whether it's crimson on the cerise side such as in the blooms of rose campion, *Lychnis coronaria*, or glowing scarlet, as found in the flower heads of *L. chalcedonica*, the Maltese cross. However, there are also pink and white forms of these species, as well as those with double-petaled flowers. Other perennial campions such as *L. flos-jovis*, with red-purple flowers and silvery leaves, and *L. viscaria*, the catchfly, are desirable too, but less commonly grown.

GROWING NOTES

Campions are meadowy plants that do best in cool and temperate climates, low humidity, and full sun. In these ideal conditions, they will flower from late spring throughout summer. The plants also adapt to warmer regions, where part shade is preferred, however, they may flower only in spring. Even the perennial species can be short-lived, but the plants freely set seed. Clumps may be divided in winter; the oldest sections should be discarded.

Perennial campions include the Maltese cross, *Lychnis chalcedonica* (left), and the rose campion, *L. coronaria* (above).

MONARDA DIDYMA

BERGAMOT

One of the few perennials to cross the fine line between the herb garden and ornamental border, bergamot is grown both for its aromatic leaves and its decorative flowers. Native to North America, it is also commonly known as bee balm (for its nectar-rich flowers), horsemint (it belongs to the mint family), and Oswego tea (named after the tribe of indigenous people who led this use of its leaves). Garden varieties of bergamot have concentrated on accentuating the plants' unusual and attractive flower forms and improving their colors—now vibrant red, crimson, pink, purple, or white.

GROWING NOTES

Suitable for most garden climates, bergamot should be planted in full sun or semi-shade, in an open position. It has a tall and rangy habit that can smother other plants if grown too close, and is also greedy for water. Bergamot is, however, herbaceous—the plant dies back, or should be cut, to ground level in winter—and therefore relatively easy to control.

An aromatic herb and an ornamental perennial, bergamot should be placed where its flowers and fragrant leaves can be enjoyed.

PAPAVER ORIENTALE
ORIENTAL POPPY

The oriental is the only poppy from this genus, *Papaver*, that is regularly cultivated as a perennial. Herbaceous in habit, the oriental poppy grows into a tall rangy clump of coarse hairy leaves and, unlike other poppies whose time is spring, produces its blooms in summer. The oriental's flowers are stunningly large and of silky iridescent colors, some with a tell-tale inky blotch at the base of each petal. Original flower forms were orange or red and black, but cultivars now also include crimson, white, or pink blooms, some with double petals, picotee edges, or frills.

GROWING NOTES

Oriental poppies prefer cool to temperate climates and are short-lived in warmer regions. They require full sun and a light, well-drained but rich soil. The plants flower from late spring through summer, and some will need staking to support their profusion of blooms. Cultivars should be propagated by division of clumps to ensure a reliable result and this is best done in winter while the plants are dormant.

Many of the oriental poppies are marked with a tell-tale inky black blotch at the base of each petal, an inheritance from the species flower.

PELARGONIUM

R egal, zonal, stellar, ivy-leaved, or scented, pelargoniums may be called by many names—but never geranium. Although from the same family, Geraniaceae, geraniums (commonly called cranesbills) and pelargoniums (erroneously called geraniums) are separate genera, distinguished mostly by flower shape, each a dynasty of its own.

The pelargonium is one of the world's most familiar plants (for geranium, see page 248), and there are countless cultivars with flowers in any color, or combination of hues, except true black or blue. As a pot plant, its popularity is unrivaled.

Probably the pelargonium best known is the zonal, *Pelargonium* x *hortorum*, which often has reddish-brown markings on a rounded leaf. The varieties available are diverse, including the stellars, with star-shaped flowers and acute leaves; flower forms such as "cactus," "carnation," or "rosebud"; and fancy-leaved zonals, with foliage variegations and colors.

The regal pelargonium, *P.* x *domesticum*, is also immensely popular and diverse. It has distinct flowers—larger, more fluted, often frilled or ruffled, with a colorful flare or feathering on each petal. Regals include near-black flowers, "miniature" forms, and the compact-growing, dainty-flowering group known as Angels.

Zonals are among the best known of pelargoniums, with both fancy leaf and flower forms, such as the "rosebud" type (right).

Other popular pelargoniums include the scented-leaf species and hybrids, with fragrant foliage reminiscent of rose, lemon, nutmeg, apple, peppermint, or coconut; as well as the ivy-leaved, *P. peltatum*, a sprawling or clambering, free-flowering and easy-growing species (and cultivars), synonymous with European window boxes.

GROWING NOTES

Pelargoniums can be cultivated in most garden climates, given suitable conditions, and gardeners everywhere may choose from a diverse range. Generally, the plants need to be kept away from frost and constant hot humidity. They prefer well-drained soil and flower better in full sun. They are easily propagated by tip cuttings, and in this way pelargonium collections can quickly evolve. For the best selection, contact one of the many pelargonium societies or specialist nurseries around the world.

Pelargoniums are synonymous with window boxes, but these plants are also very adaptable to gardens.

PENSTEMON SPECIES & CULTIVARS
PENSTEMON

This all-American beauty has become one of the world's favorite perennials, gracing borders and cottage gardens with its easy-growing habits and vividly colored tubular flowers. But while there are about 250 species of penstemon from various habitats in North America, ranging from low-growing rockery or alpine plants only 4 in (10 cm) in height to the tall meadowy types with 3 ft (1 m) high flower stems, it is the modern cultivars and hybrids which are most commonly grown.

The modern garden penstemons can have flowers that are darkest red or deep purple, bright pink or lilac-blue, through all the pastel shades of these colors to pure white. The flower corollas may be finely funneled, or bell-like and elegant, or bicolored and flouncy. The plants are generally evergreen, with lance-shaped leaves, and they flower from late spring throughout summer.

Penstemons may be planted in dense drifts or mixed in borders. Racemes of flowers are produced from late spring throughout summer.

Tubular flowers are typical of all penstemons: some are finely funneled on slender stems, while others are frilled and fancy.

GROWING NOTES

Due to their various origins, penstemon cultivars and hybrids are adaptable to many climates from warm to cool, though they dislike tropical environments and they may become herbaceous and die back during frosty episodes. The plants also prefer full sun, shelter from strong wind, and very well drained soil—root rot through overwatering or poor drainage is the bane of all penstemons and the rockery or alpine types are especially susceptible.

Penstemons can be short-lived in the garden, but removing flower stems as they finish will prolong the season of blooms, and cutting off old growth at ground level in the fall will help to rejuvenate the plants. Penstemons can be grown from seed or cuttings or by division of established clumps.

PENTAS LANCEOLATA
PENTAS

T he verdant leaves and exotic colors of pentas bring a touch of the tropics to the garden. With copious clusters of star-shaped flowers, produced from early spring throughout the warmer months to early winter, and a dense shrub-like habit of large ovate leaves, this plant looks lush. *Pentas lanceolata* originates from Africa and the Middle East, and is sometimes known as Egyptian star cluster. Several cultivars are available, varying in flower color: these include many shades of pink, magenta, red, white, and two-tones.

Pentas may bloom for most of the year; cutting flowers for the vase will help to prolong the plant's flowering season.

GROWING NOTES

Pentas prefer warm or tropical garden climates (they don't tolerate any frost or low winter temperatures) but can also be grown as potted plants indoors. In the garden, the plants require full sun, at least for half the day, shelter from strong wind, and well-drained, organically enriched soil. To make the most of the long flowering season, cut back entire stems of finished blooms in winter and spring, and trim only the flower heads in summer and fall.

PHYSOSTEGIA VIRGINIANA
OBEDIENT PLANT

The obedient plant blooms from midsummer through fall. Its flowers are fascinatingly mobile, and stems can be cut for arrangements.

The common name of this herbaceous perennial, a native of North America, refers to the curious compliancy of its flowers—attached to the terminal stem by a hinge-like stalk, the flowers may be moved on their swiveling pedicels and they will then stay rearranged. Regardless of its novelty value, the obedient plant provides outstanding color in the garden. The flower stems are quite tall, up to 3 ft (1 m) in height, and plentiful, with blooms of magenta, red or white. The plant itself only grows to about 6 in (15 cm) but spreads, vigorously, by stolons (runners) to form a large clump in a single season.

GROWING NOTES

The obedient plant is very adaptable to sun or part shade, and will grow in all garden climates except the tropics. It requires very little maintenance in the garden, except the removal of spent flowers and trimming of foliage as the plant becomes dormant in winter. Divide the clumps to propagate plants or to keep them controlled.

POTENTILLA SPECIES & CULTIVARS
CINQUEFOIL

Belonging to the rose family, *Potentilla* is an extensive genus of about 500 naturally occurring species, including annuals, perennials, and small shrubs, but there are also many selected cultivars and hybrids. In the garden, the perennial types are among the most commonly grown and they can range from rockery plants, only 4 in (10 cm) in height, to border types more than 2 ft (60 cm) tall. Their flowers are usually small but plentiful and can have single or double petals. Red-flowered hybrids only appeared a few decades ago, and have led a new wave of flower colors, including intense orange and intricate pink and red vignettes.

Flowering in late spring or summer, the many perennial types of *Potentilla* include the modern red-flowered hybrids.

GROWING NOTES

Depending on the species, the perennial types of *Potentilla* can be herbaceous or evergreen. They all grow in cool to warm climates, preferring full sun in cooler regions and part shade in warmer gardens. Soil must be well drained, but plants will need to be regularly watered in hot weather as they are quick to wilt. The hybrids should be propagated only by division of clumps, and this is easily done in winter.

STOKESIA LAEVIS
STOKES' ASTER

Like all members of the daisy family to which it belongs, the Stokes' aster has composite flower heads formed by a complex arrangement of florets. In this genus, however, the ray florets are deeply divided, giving the flower heads a shimmering, fringed appearance. *Stokesia laevis*, native to south-eastern North America, has natural flower colors that are bright pink, purple, and mauve, but cultivars with lilac-blue, pastel pink, or white blooms are also available. Stokes' aster makes an impact in masses on its own, but also mixes well with other plants, and can be grown in containers.

Stokes' aster flowers from early summer to late fall; deeply divided florets give the blooms a fringed appearance.

GROWING NOTES
Stokes' aster prefers warm to subtropical climates, where it behaves as an evergreen. The plants also grow in cooler areas but tend to be herbaceous, dying down in winter. They need full sun, with some shade in warm gardens, and protection from strong wind. Divide clumps in late winter or early spring, or propagate from root cuttings. Remove blooms to prolong the plant's flowering; the cut flowers last well in arrangements.

Perennial verbenas may flower continuously from early spring to late fall, especially if the finished flower heads are removed.

VERBENA SPECIES & HYBRIDS
VERVAIN

Ornamentally, most of the perennial forms of *Verbena* are trailing plants with bright green, dramatically dissected leaves and clusters of vividly colored flowers that are produced throughout the warmer months of the year. Many hybrids exist and continue to develop, though some of these are best as annuals. The fantastic flower colors now include red, magenta, pink, purple, white, bicolors, and vignettes, with some cultivars having clusters of various tones. The plants are generally low-growing, with an informal tumbling habit, and easy to maintain; they are ideal as ground cover, on steep slopes, in low borders or raised beds, and also in pots.

GROWING NOTES
The perennial vervains generally prefer warm, frost-free climates, though they will tolerate quite low winter temperatures and also tropical conditions. They require full sun, though some shade in hot situations is appreciated. Water plants regularly during spring and summer. Some cultivars become straggly and unproductive after a few years; however, they are easily replaced, propagated by cuttings or division.

ROSA SPECIES & CULTIVARS

rose

The rose is more than just a flower, more than a plant, more than a garden. The rose is a symbol, universal, with a language of its own that everyone can speak. As Gertrude Stein said, "Rose is a rose is a rose."

In the garden, we are devoted to the rose. We worship the ground in which they grow—in pots and on patios, in formal beds, and border upon border. We plant them in our most sacred spaces, close to our homes, in our cemeteries, around our churches, mosques, and temples (the rose knows no divisions). Everyone loves a rose, and those who don't simply haven't met the right one.

Of course, there are many roses for us to love. Apart from the species (often known as "wild roses"), some of the roses in cultivation are very, very old. Like the damasks (*Rosa* x *damascena*) which were introduced to northern Europe by the Crusaders, or 'Omar Khayyám' named after the Persian poet (circa 1048–1122? CE) and reputed to derive from a plant growing on his grave. The terms "heritage" or "old-garden" are used to cover many of these roses.

The "modern" roses include some of the milestones in gardening history. The hybrid tea, created in the 19th century, is one of these. Until the recent interest in antiquity, the hybrid tea was *the* garden rose. It is the ancestor of most modern roses, and among the hybrid teas is the most widely grown rose in the world—'Peace'—developed around the time of the Second World War, and just as popular today.

Clockwise from top left: the species *Rosa chinensis*; the bourbon 'La Reine Victoria'; and the climbers 'Pierre de Ronsard' and 'Altissimo'.

The old-garden tea rose 'Duchesse de Brabant' has soft pink blooms, and the hybrid perpetual 'Reines des Violettes' is deep magenta-red.

In the last 50 years or so, a new age of roses has dawned. Now, there are roses out there in every color, except true black, green, or blue, and many specific to gardeners' needs, including miniatures, ground covers, and the patio, floribunda, and polyantha-types which have taken off as potted color. The "English" rose has been remodeled, too, thanks mostly to the efforts of David Austin and his many free-flowering, fragrant and multi-petaled rose forms.

True rose lovers hold that the official plant type is irrelevant—what is important is the rose. Gardeners should take note and simply choose the plants that best suit their conditions and the flowers they like most.

GROWING NOTES

Wild roses occur naturally in the northern hemisphere from the Arctic to the tropics, so there really is a rose for any garden situation. In their right climates, roses are very easy to grow and some will even thrive indefinitely without attention. Their main requirement is full sun, all day, for best growth and flowering. The soil should be well drained and heavily enriched with aged organic material before planting (acidic soils should be balanced, too). The plants need good air

Clockwise from top left: the English rose 'Graham Thomas'; the hybrid tea 'Double Delight'; the noisette rambler 'Lamarque'; and the floribunda 'Pink Iceberg.'

'Albertine' has very

fragrant flowers in

midsummer; this

vigorous climber is

grown here as an

informal hedge.

circulation but protect them from very strong wind which ruins the flowers. Regular feeding promotes prolific plants, but most roses will flower anyway: a general guide is to feed in early spring, then after the first flush of flowers, and again around midsummer. Pruning depends greatly on the type of rose—some require traditional-style pruning, while others barely need a light trim. The text-book pruning is usually done in late winter or early spring, but many roses—old and new—can be simply trimmed at any time by removing the finished flowers and dead stems. Most roses strike easily from cuttings taken in late winter or early spring (prunings will usually do), though some are not vigorous if they aren't grafted onto understocks. Pests and diseases must be controlled for roses to perform their best, but in recent years many breeders have concentrated on the plants' resistance to these problems.

Gardeners who get hooked on roses should join a club or society; talk to other growers; read books (no plant has inspired more titles); and, most importantly, get in touch with specialist nurseries who can supply them with top-of-the-range plants—a rose can last longer than a gardener's lifetime, so it's wise to start with the best.

warm

W
arm colors are everywhere in the world of plants— in the petals of some flowers, in stamens, in fruit and seed, in stems and trunks, but also in the autumnal tones of dying leaves or the faded hues of finished blooms. Warm, too, are the colors of the earth and the sun. So with very little effort, in all the seasons, warm colors naturally create a rich tapestry.

Warm colors have a wide tonal range, from pale moonlight yellow to burning orange-red, yet they blend seamlessly together. PREVIOUS PAGES: *Gazania* x *hybrida*.

Warm colors are based on yellow, nature's own highlight. From bright and luminous or golden to orange, bronze, and all the simmering infusions of red—warm-colored flowers are outstanding features but also play off each other's subtleties. They are enriched by lush green backgrounds or by foliage toned yellow or brown, and brightened by a hot splash of purple, red, or blue.

Warm-colored flowers always brighten the garden, but these tones are also very easy to incorporate in many styles and designs, being natural complements of green. RIGHT: Yellow coneflowers, *Rudbeckia laciniata*.

In this chapter, we have featured flowering perennials in warm colors. Some are intrinsically flowers of summer and the sun, only found in yellow or gold. Others, like the daylily or chrysanthemum, feature warm hues in their extensive color range. Note that warm colors can also be closely related to pastels or hot tones, and they have many flowering perennials in common.

A garden tapestry of warm tones, interweaving annuals, perennials, and shrubs, is welcoming in all the seasons. FOLLOWING PAGES: A design composed of warm-colored flowering perennials highlighted by structural foliage.

ABUTILON X HYBRIDUM
LANTERN FLOWER

Abutilon x hybridum is very adaptable in gardens and flower colors may be glowing red, orange, or yellow, as well as pastel pink or white.

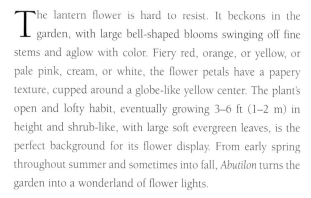

The lantern flower is hard to resist. It beckons in the garden, with large bell-shaped blooms swinging off fine stems and aglow with color. Fiery red, orange, or yellow, or pale pink, cream, or white, the flower petals have a papery texture, cupped around a globe-like yellow center. The plant's open and lofty habit, eventually growing 3–6 ft (1–2 m) in height and shrub-like, with large soft evergreen leaves, is the perfect background for its flower display. From early spring throughout summer and sometimes into fall, *Abutilon* turns the garden into a wonderland of flower lights.

GROWING NOTES

All lantern flower species originate in warm and tropical areas, mainly South America, and so prefer these climates. The hybrids, *Abutilon* x *hybridum*, however, are very adaptable to much cooler regions. They prefer full sun, to part shade only in hot climates, and protection from strong wind. Remove flowers as they finish and occasionally trim to keep plants in shape; prune plants that become rangy to encourage compact growth and more flowers.

ALSTROEMERIA SPECIES & HYBRIDS

PERUVIAN LILY

Favored by florists for its tall straight stems of flamboyantly marked and long-lasting flowers, the Peruvian lily is cultivated on a wide scale, both commercially and in the garden. Also known as the lily of the Incas, most species of Peruvian lily actually originate from Chile, including *Alstroemeria aurantiaca* (syn. *A. aurea*), with flowers in a range of orange and yellow tones, and *A. ligtu*, with blooms that are lavender, pink, or red. Colorful hybrids, of course, abound—exploring the spectrum of streaks, spots, and tones, as well as enhancing petal frills and flares. And while many of these remain in the province of commercial cultivators, for most gardeners, the easily accessible range is spectacular enough.

Most of the Peruvian lilies grown in gardens are hybrids. These can have a long flowering season throughout spring and summer or from summer to fall.

The flowers of Peruvian lilies range from softest cream and pink, tinged with green, through all the warm tones of yellow and orange to rich reds and purples.

The Peruvian lily is a herbaceous perennial that grows from fleshy rhizomes with tall stems, usually 1–2 ft (30–60 cm) in height, bearing narrow lance-shaped leaves. Flower stems are mostly produced from spring through summer or from summer to fall, depending on the type. In suitable conditions, the plants eventually form large drifting clumps but they also mix well in borders and thrive in pots.

GROWING NOTES

Peruvian lilies will grow in most climates from warm to cool, though they are unsuitable for the tropics, and are best in greenhouses in very cold areas. Depending on the climate, they may prefer full sun or slight shade. The plants require shelter from strong wind and well-drained, enriched soil, but do not overfeed them as this inhibits the blooms. Water regularly in spring and summer, then reduce after flowering. Whether cutting flowers for the vase, or when they are finished, remove the stems at ground level. Many types will grow from seed, but dividing clumps is easier.

ANIGOZANTHOS SPECIES & CULTIVARS

KANGAROO PAW

The kangaroo paw is a flower like no other. A botanical curiosity with colorful furry petals, it originates only in Western Australia, and even so the genus is limited to a south-west region. Here, the plants often grow in vast sunny meadows creating a haze of iridescent color, with flowers that are blazing yellow or orange, or an amazing red and metallic green. Likewise in the garden, the kangaroo paw, with its evergreen strappy leaves, is spectacular in drifts or bold clumps; but also makes an outstanding container specimen. Modern cultivars are particularly successful, and their flowers may be red, pink, yellow, orange, green, or near gold.

GROWING NOTES

Kangaroo paws, especially the new hybrids, are adaptable to most warm to cool climates, though ideal regions have hot, dry summers and cool, wet winters (Mediterranean-style). The plants must have full sun; very well drained soil, preferably sandy or gravelly; and regular watering during the growing season. Cut flower stems at ground level to encourage new growth. Divide established clumps to propagate.

Kangaroo paws flower in spring and summer. The flowers are long-lasting on the plant or when cut for arrangements.

ANTHEMIS TINCTORIA
YELLOW CHAMOMILE

Closely related to the culinary herb of the same common name, this evergreen perennial is also known as dyer's chamomile because a yellow dye can be extracted from its flowers. In the garden, the plants are also much valued for their color—shining golden yellow in the species, but also lemon or white in cultivars—with the flowers produced in masses for many months, from spring throughout summer and sometimes into fall. Native to Europe and western Asia, *Anthemis tinctoria* grows in vigorous mounds, about 1–2 ft (30–60 cm) in height, of fragrant feathery foliage. In groups, the yellow chamomile can be used as ground covers or to create informal drifts, but, being easy to restrain, they also mix well with other plants in borders.

GROWING NOTES

Very easy to grow in most climates from warm to cool (but not the tropics), yellow chamomile requires full sun and well-drained soil. It does tolerate poor soils, and also infrequent watering once established. Plants can be short-lived, but are easily renewed from cuttings or divisions.

Yellow chamomile grows in feathery drifts of fragrant leaves; there are also cultivars with lemon or white flowers.

AQUILEGIA SPECIES & CULTIVARS
COLUMBINE

With uniquely spurred and hooded flowers, in an infinitely evolving range of colors and color combinations, the columbine, a wildflower of the northern hemisphere, has fascinated gardeners for centuries.

Yet even though the genus *Aquilegia* is widely distributed in the wild—from Spain to Siberia, or from Canada to Mexico—only a few species are commonly grown in gardens. This is partly because columbines cross readily between themselves, so there are naturally occurring variations and hybrids galore. But also because the European wildflower *A. vulgaris*, in all its glorious forms, has dominated the columbine scene.

Increasingly favored though (perhaps a sign of our times) are the blue-flowered species, such as *A. alpina* and *A. caerulea*, the floral emblem of Colorado. Also becoming popular and accessible is the related genus *Semiaquilegia*, which is very similar to the columbine but has a loftier habit of tall wiry stems, branched and bearing dainty bell-shaped blooms.

Flowering in spring or summer, most of the garden columbines, *Aquilegia* x *hybrida*, derive from the European wildflower, *A. vulgaris*.

Columbines, with their distinct flowers and soft clumps of ferny foliage, are favorites of cottage gardens, woodlands, pots, and borders. The flower stems are also long-lasting in arrangements.

GROWING NOTES

Columbines, having varied origins, are very adaptable to all climates except the tropics or dry inland areas. They are usually herbaceous perennials, but may be grown as annuals in warmer gardens. Mostly the plants prefer light shade, either morning sun only or filtered all day (such as under deciduous trees), but in cooler areas they like full sun. The soil should be well drained, and heavily enriched with organic material. Clumps are not easily divided, but this is the only sure method of propagating plants exactly. Seeds, of course, are produced prolifically (remove flowers to control production) and though the resulting plants are variable, surprise is one of the columbine's charms.

ARCTOTIS SPECIES & HYBRIDS
AURORA DAISY

The aurora daisy in full bloom is a summer color spectacular, with the plant's sprawling drift of gray-green leaves covered in radiant flowers. In the species, *Arctotis acaulis*, which originates in southern Africa (and, like many others in the family, is also known as the African daisy), the flower heads are deep orange to cinnabar red, but the hybrids, *A. x hybrida*, also include those with white, creamy yellow, or pink blooms. All the aurora daisies have long tapered ray florets (these provide the brilliant color); and central discs of intricately patterned bands of black, yellow, or gold—sometimes in dazzling combinations.

Aurora daisies have brightly colored ray florets, but they can also feature intricately patterned central discs in black and gold.

GROWING NOTES

Aurora daisies grow in most climates, but prefer those with low humidity, and are not suitable for tropical areas. The plants must have full sun all day, both for vigorous growth and for the flowers to open. They also need well-drained soil, preferably sandy, and are very suitable for banks or slopes. *Arctotis* species and hybrids can be short-lived in gardens, often flowering best in their first year.

AURINIA SAXATILIS
GOLDEN TUFT

Also appropriately known as gold dust, this tuft-forming ground-hugging perennial originates in the stony mountain habitats of Europe and western Asia, making it ideal for raised gardens, slopes, and rockeries. Growing in dense rosettes of lance-shaped, slightly hairy leaves, the plants can also be featured in troughs and large containers. They mix well with other perennials, shrubs, or trees, and are naturally complemented by materials such as terracotta, cement, or stone. The wild species *Aurinia saxatilis* (syn. *Alyssum saxatile*) has gleaming, rich yellow flowers, but some cultivars have white, cream, or lemon-yellow blooms and there is also a variegated foliage form with ivory-edged leaves.

Golden tuft flowers in spring; each rounded cluster is composed of many tiny blooms.

GROWING NOTES

These evergreen perennials prefer cool to cold climates, but will also adapt to more temperate regions. The plants must have full sun in an open position and free-draining soil—poor-quality soils are tolerated but not those that are waterlogged. Trim off finished flowers (use shears) to keep plants nicely rounded and productive.

BULBINELLA FLORIBUNDA
GOLDEN WAND LILY

The golden wand lily eventually grows into a theatrical clump; flares of color are formed by starry flowers that open slowly along the spire.

The dramatic pyrotechnic effect of the golden wand lily is created by tiny starry flowers that open successively along a tapering spire. The flare of color lasts several weeks, starting in late winter or early spring, while the stem grows ever taller and bands of flowers peak then expire (leaving cute gold dots where they had been). A native of South Africa, from a small genus within the lily family, *Bulbinella floribunda* grows from a fleshy tuberous rhizome into a tangle of long, succulent grass-like leaves. In the garden, the plants are best left to develop into large informal clumps so that their towering flower stems can be most theatrically displayed.

GROWING NOTES

The golden wand lily grows well in cool to warm climates, but isn't suitable for the tropics, and prefers areas of high winter rainfall, replicating its natural habitat. The plants require full sun, but part shade in warm gardens is tolerated. Soil should be well drained but enriched with organic matter. Water plants generously during the growing season (usually beginning late fall). Remove flower stems as they finish.

CANNA SPECIES & CULTIVARS
CANNA

Like dancing flames, the flowers, and sometimes also the leaves, of cannas ignite the garden in summer. Cannas don't bloom, they blaze. In the tropical wild, the species, such as *Canna edulis* (syn. *C. indica*), mostly bear small red or orange flowers, but in our gardens the modern hybrids, *C.* x *generalis*, have huge blooms of spectacular hues—intense reds and yellows to near-pastel pinks and apricots, as well as whites, and bicolors splashed or speckled with contrasting tones.

The leaves of cannas, elegantly tapered and normally in a range of fluid greens, are ornamental in their own right and there are varieties grown purely for their colorful foliage—some are dark purple or burgundy, others are patterned bronze, or may be finely striped red, copper, or gold. While canna flowers aren't suitable for floristry arrangements, the leaves are widely used and admired.

GROWING NOTES
Cannas have tropical origins and are evergreen in warm climates where they enjoy sunny positions tempered by part

Modern hybrid cannas, *Canna* x *generalis*, include flame-like flower colors that ignite the garden throughout summer.

shade in extreme heat. The plants also grow well in cooler areas, in full sun, but the rhizomes become dormant in winter. Cannas require a rich and permanently moist soil, with plenty of water during the growing season. They love marshy marginal conditions, such as on the edges of ponds, and will also grow in shallow water.

The plants can range in height from 2 ft (60 cm) to more than 6 ft (2 m) and will form dense clumps over time. After flowering, remove finished stems at ground level. In cool climates, the leaves will naturally die back for winter and the crown of the plant should be mulched with straw or, if frosts are severe, the rhizomes may need to be lifted and stored. Prune the leaves of evergreen cannas at the end of winter to invigorate the plants.

Cannas planted in drifts or clumps look most effective. Among those grown for ornamental foliage are striped variations, striking and surreal.

CHRYSANTHEMUM X MORIFOLIUM
CHRYSANTHEMUM

The chrysanthemum as gardeners know it (although it is sometimes called the florists' chrysanthemum) goes back more than 2,500 years to ancient China, where the species *Chrysanthemum morifolium* originates and was first cultivated. At some indistinct time, possibly around the start of the Christian Era, the chrysanthemum crossed over to Japan where it was fervently embraced (the Japanese were holding chrysanthemum shows more than a thousand years ago). So, by the time the plant found its way to Europe, around the 17th century, hundreds of cultivars had already been established in China and Japan. And while other species have contributed to the flowers' fame, none has been as significant as *C. morifolium*, from which thousands of hybrids have sprung.

With an ever-increasing range of types, the chrysanthemums' classification has been complicated. Currently, they exclusively occupy the genus *Chrysanthemum,* and all related plants have been assigned new names. Specialist societies and nurseries (of which there is a multitude worldwide) have also developed a

The are so many forms of chrysanthemums that the plants are defined by their flower types. The quilled flower (left) is also known as spider.

The natural flowering season of garden chrysanthemums is the fall, though potted plants in bloom are available year round.

common language to describe the many cultivars, based on flower type; these include single, pompom, anemone-centred, reflexing, incurved, and spider or quilled.

GROWING NOTES

In the garden, all the chrysanthemums require similar conditions—full sun, with protection from strong wind, and well-drained, very rich soil. They will grow in cool to warm climates, but not tropical. Flowering potted plants are available all year round (induced by commercial growers who fiddle with the hours of "daylight"), but the normal flowering time of garden-grown chrysanthemums is the fall, as they only produce flowers after midsummer, when days become shorter. Once flowering is finished, the plants should be cut back to about 6 in (15 cm) above ground level; those in pots should be transplanted to the garden.

CLIVIA MINIATA
CLIVIA

Clivias light up shady gardens with their flowers in late winter or spring; the flower stems can be cut for arrangements, too.

Few plants flower so brilliantly in the shade as the clivias. In low-light conditions, the ember-orange of the bell-shaped flowers, against the dark green foliage, really glows. Conversely, this evergreen perennial from South Africa suffers in the sun: its broad, fleshy strap leaves are easily scorched, and the flowers fade to washed-out tones. Although *Clivia miniata* is immensely popular, and despite the efforts of plant breeders, the flower color has eluded artificial change—varying only slightly from bright shades of orange to cinnabar red. Recently, however, a yellow-flowered cultivar 'Aurea' has appeared on the world market, as well as a cream-flowered one with variegated leaves. Both are rare and expensive, and so the popularity of the species remains unchallenged.

GROWING NOTES

Clivias are incredibly tough and adaptable to all climates which aren't affected by heavy frost. They thrive in a wide range of soils and shady conditions (from heavy to lightly dappled), including under trees, and may be grown in pots. The plants grow from rhizomes into clumps that can be divided for propagation.

COREOPSIS SPECIES & CULTIVARS

COREOPSIS

The coreopsis has no sense of restraint: it flowers as if it were the only thing under the sun—in abundance, and with boundless joy. The wild coreopsis, with uniformly yellow blooms, may be common in the fields of its native United States, but in the garden these herbaceous members of the daisy family hold their own among the best of flowering perennials. They grow easily and flower unceasingly from spring throughout summer. There are many ornamental species and cultivars of coreopsis, including dwarf forms, those that have flower heads with dark contrasting centers, or blooms with deeply serrated or double ray petals.

GROWING NOTES

Coreopsis thrives in an open position, basking in full sun. It tolerates some shade, but flowering is less profuse; rich soils and overwatering have the same disappointing effect. Growing in dense clumps, the plants, once established, are very resistant to drought. Remove finished stems to prolong the flowering season and to keep plants compact. Coreopsis is easily grown from seed or by dividing clumps.

Ornamental forms of coreopsis include those with double ray petals (above); and *Coreopsis tinctoria* (left), a species with two-tone blooms.

DIETES BICOLOR

Appearing throughout spring and summer, the symmetrical flowers of *Dietes bicolor* have a luminous color quality.

The symmetry of its six buttery petals and trio of burgundy blotches (whichever way you look at it from above) is an intriguing flower feature of the yellow dietes. Endemic to South Africa, *Dietes bicolor* comes from a small genus that includes the more common *D. grandiflora*, with lilac and white flowers, to which it is closely related. These evergreens of the iris family have stiff, upright strap leaves that taper sharply, and grow from a rhizome to form a fanned clump. Each bloom lasts only a day or two, but the flower stems bear many buds and each plant produces multiple stems so that flowering continues uninterrupted throughout the warm seasons.

GROWING NOTES

Easily grown in climates from cool to subtropical, dietes, once established, will survive and flower through the harshest conditions including strong wind, steep banks, poor soil, pollution, and drought. They are spectacularly successful in large-scale landscaping. Do not remove flower stems, as they produce blooms over many seasons. Clumps may be divided but are slow to re-establish.

EURYOPS PECTINATUS
EURYOPS

Even though its blooms begin to appear in winter, the euryops flowers as if it was summer, in a burst of bright sunshine yellow that brings quiet gardens to life. Native to South Africa, *Euryops pectinatus* has deeply cut gray-green leaves and grows into a shrub-like mound, up to about 3 ft (1 m) high and wide—a cheerful sight when covered in flowers while the season is still cool. Like most members of the daisy family, this evergreen is also very easy to grow: euryops will thrive in low-maintenance borders, rockeries, containers, windy sites, and seaside gardens.

GROWING NOTES

Euryops grows in most climates, except the extremely hot, tropical, or cold. The plants require full sun to flower prolifically, and also prefer well-drained soil. Once established, they tolerate dry periods, but occasional deep watering will be appreciated. While the plants are fairly long-lived, they are most productive in their early years, especially if cut back hard after flowering. Propagate from cuttings in the fall.

The flowers of euryops bring summer color to the winter garden; removing finished flowers ensures a long display until late spring.

GAILLARDIA SPECIES & HYBRIDS

BLANKET FLOWER

Some of the best-colored blanket flowers can be found in the perennial hybrids; all *Gaillardia* blooms are very suitable for cutting.

The blanket flower loves the sun. The plants thrive best in sunny conditions, and their flower heads are among the brightest of summer, in radiant yellow, orange, red, and gold, often with the colors in circular bands. A small genus of daisies, from the United States and South America, *Gaillardia* is comprised of annuals and perennials that grow in small basal clumps of gray-green leaves. And while a few species, such as the perennial *G. aristata,* with yellow and red-centered flower heads, are quite common, the hybrids and cultivars are more popular. The hybrid *G.* x *grandiflora* includes some of the best-colored blanket flowers, such as 'Burgundy,' with dark red blooms edged in bands of gold, and 'Goblin,' a dwarf form.

GROWING NOTES

Blanket flowers grow in most climates, except the tropics. They do require full sun, and well-drained light soil, but also tolerate infrequent watering once established. The perennials can be short-lived; however, they are easily propagated by division or cuttings.

Most of the gazanias grown in gardens are *Gazania* x *hybrida*: their flower range is inspiring and new colors and combinations will frequently appear.

GAZANIA SPECIES & HYBRIDS
GAZANIA

The gazania is among the most creative of flowers. From just a few species, endemic to South Africa, with mainly orange or yellow blooms, this daisy-like perennial has developed an array of flower variations—many occurring naturally, without human intervention, in gardens and in the wild. The gazania flower may be red as the desert sun, dawn pink, or pale as bleached sand—with bands black as night, starry dots, bright stripes, or light flares. With unbounded imagination, these flowers match magenta with beige, or dark brown with soft pink, or place bold black splashes over gold.

And yet this ground-covering evergreen is one of the toughest plants to grace the garden. With narrow lance-shaped and weather-resistant gray-green leaves, forming thick basal clumps, gazanias can be successfully planted in coastal regions, on sand banks to stabilize seaside areas, or on windy, rocky cliffs. They also adapt well to the urban jungle, thriving beside highways and in streetscapes, along footpaths, in rockeries and pots, and on balconies and rooftops.

GROWING NOTES

Most gazanias in cultivation are hybrids, *Gazania* x *hybrida*, with many derived from the species *G. rigens* which has orange or yellow flowers and sometimes black or white markings. All gazanias are easy to grow in various climates, from cool to warm, or arid to subtropical. They must have full sun all day (the flowers don't open without it) and very well drained soil. Do not overfeed or overwater these plants—they thrive, and are most floriferous, in unpampered conditions. Gazanias are very easily propagated by division or cuttings, but self-seeding is more exciting, having the potential of producing flowers in colors or combinations unknown.

Gazanias thrive in tough conditions, such as in seaside gardens or hot rockeries—but also in the urban jungle, along walls, in pots, and on rooftops and balconies.

HEDYCHIUM SPECIES
GINGER LILY

Mostly from temperate and tropical parts of Asia, but also Madagascar, these evergreens are related to culinary ginger (from the family Zingiberaceae). Rather than being grown for their rhizomes, the ginger lilies are valued for their striking and highly scented flowers. The huge broad leaves are lusciously ornamental, too, and in ideal situations, the plants can reach 6 ft (2 m) in height. Garden species include the kahili ginger (*Hedychium gardnerianum*), with its intensely aromatic yellow flowers and very vigorous growth; the white ginger or garland flower (*H. coronarium*), with white blooms also very fragrant; and the scarlet ginger lily (*H. coccineum*), which has red, pink, or salmon-orange flowers.

GROWING NOTES

All ginger lilies grow best in warm-temperate to tropical gardens, requiring greenhouse conditions in frost-affected climates. The plants prefer sheltered, partly shaded positions in rich moist soil and generous watering throughout the growing season. Cutting back the plant to ground level after flowering has finished, or in winter, will encourage new growth in spring.

Fragrant ginger lilies flower in late summer and fall; the kahili ginger, with striking red stamens and yellow petals, is one of the most vigorous.

HELENIUM AUTUMNALE
SNEEZEWEED

The flower heads of *Helenium* are among the most richly colored of the daisies. Its ray florets are flared and divided, like a twirling skirt of coppery red, tawny orange, or yellow-gold. The conical center may be bronzed, burgundy, or dark brown, with a chorus of tiny golden florets that transform it into a glowing globe. Native to the open marshy meadows of North America, these tall-growing herbaceous perennials are especially effective when planted in dramatic drifts or clumps that take advantage of their summer and fall colors.

The flower display of *Helenium* lasts from late summer to fall. 'Bruno' (above) and 'Moerheim Beauty' (right) are among the most popular cultivars.

GROWING NOTES

Most sneezeweeds prefer cool climates, but will adapt to warmer regions. The plants require full sun all day, and moist rich soil with regular watering during the growing seasons. Remove finished stems to prolong flowering (the blooms are excellent for arrangements), and cut back foliage after it dies down. Mature plants may be divided for propagation, but discard the old central part of the clump.

HELIOPSIS HELIANTHOIDES
HELIOPSIS

The botanical name *Heliopsis* translates as "resembling the sun," an apt description for the golden-yellow flowerheads of these perennials. Originating from the prairies of North America, there are only about a dozen species of heliopsis, with one in common cultivation. *Heliopsis helianthoides* (the species name means "like a sunflower") is herbaceous and tall-growing, to about 5 ft (1.5 m) in height, and up to 3 ft (1 m) wide. The plants have coarse hairy leaves and strong panicles of large yellow flower heads (these are long-lasting when cut for the vase). Cultivars include the double-flowered and slightly shorter-growing 'Light of Loddon,' and 'Patula,' which has semi-double orange blooms.

GROWING NOTES

Heliopsis will grow in most climates, except the tropics. They require well-drained soil, enriched to encourage growth, and full sun to flower best. Remove finished flower heads to promote further blooms, and then cut the stems at ground level after all flowering is over. Heliopsis tends to be short-lived, but clumps are easily divided and plants may also be propagated from cuttings or seed.

Flowers of the sun, heliopsis have a long season of blooms from summer to fall.

HEMEROCALLIS CULTIVARS
DAYLILY

In the garden, daylilies may flower in spring, summer or fall, depending on the cultivar. There are thousands of daylily cultivars available.

The daylily is one of the most remarkable plants in cultivation. It ranks among the few influential flowers that inspire specialist nurseries, societies, shows, florists, and gardeners—worldwide. In the United States, the Hemerocallis Society is one of the country's strongest gardening organizations; while the international Hemerocallis Society registers hundreds of new daylily cultivars each year, amounting to a cornucopia of flower colors.

With so many daylilies in cultivation, official categories have evolved: the plants are classed by habit (evergreen, semi-evergreen, deciduous); then by size (dwarf, medium, tall); and finally by flowering season (early, mid, late). There are, of course, flower colors and plant forms to suit any garden design. With their large clumps of grass-like leaves, these perennials are very adaptable and easy to grow. Some cultivars can be grown in pots; others live long in the garden. There's

Though the flowers are one-day wonders, each flowering stem bears many blooms and each plant produces many stems, so the daylily's display goes on for weeks.

only one thing that the plant breeders haven't been able to improve, try as they might—the flower of the daylily refuses to remain open for more than a single day.

GROWING NOTES

Daylilies can be grown in almost all climates, except the tropics. The plants prefer full sun, but will tolerate part shade in warmer gardens. They grow in many types of soil, can be used in landscaping to stabilize banks or slopes, and also thrive in streetscapes. Once established, daylilies are very tolerant of dry seasons, though they flower better with regular watering. Remove the stems at ground level after all the flowers are finished. The clumps may be divided in late winter or early spring for propagation.

While some cultivars remain exclusively in the province of commercial floristry, an enormous range of daylilies is easily accessible to gardeners through the many specialist nurseries and societies worldwide.

HYPERICUM SPECIES & CULTIVARS
HYPERICUM

In common, the hypericums all have yellow, five-petaled cupped flowers with prominent stamens, but the genus varies greatly in habit, from low-growing prostrate forms to bushy shrubs. The best-known species is *Hypericum perforatum*, St John's wort, the herb full of magical and medicinal qualities and reputed in folklore to drive all sorts of evil spirits away. But for ornamental purposes, the upright-growing perennial *H. patulum* is often favored; as is the ground-covering rose of Sharon (*H. calycinum*). There are also many hybrids and cultivars of hypericums available, all with long seasons of flower.

GROWING NOTES
Hypericums are generally easy to grow, and adaptable to most climates except the hot tropics. Most prefer well-drained soil and full sun, though some, like the rose of Sharon, appreciate part shade when in warm gardens. Shrub types may be lightly pruned to keep them compact, and perennials bearing panicles should have spent flower stems removed. Some species will grow from seed, but cultivars and hybrids should be propagated from cuttings or by division.

The many perennial hypericums include species and cultivars, from ground covers to shrubs and tall meadow types.

Torch lilies bloom in spring, summer or fall; each spire has hundreds of flowers which open and close over several weeks.

KNIPHOFIA SPECIES & CULTIVARS
TORCH LILY

For centuries the torch lily has inspired great garden designs. Many are based on gardeners' visions (imagined or otherwise) of thousands of torch lilies blazing across the mountain grasslands of the plants' South African home, replicated in cultivation in expansive drifts. Other gardeners like their torch lilies up close and personal, in pots or bold clumps, so that the spectacle of flowers is more intimately revealed. Sometimes the plants are simply framed, such as against a wild backdrop, or creatively placed to surprise. Wherever it grows, the torch lily sets the garden alight.

Much of the popularity of the torch lily, also known as red hot poker (a likely remnant of colonial days), is due to the increasing availability of cultivars and hybrids. Most of the well-known species, such as *Kniphofia uvaria*, flower in hot red and yellow, strong colors which are not always easily placed in gardens; but the cultivars can be colored cream, orange, gold,

or light green, and include many two-tone combinations (created by the contrasting colors of the buds and flowers). Also among them are dwarf forms, up to about 2 ft (60 cm) in height, and ideal for smaller gardens and tubs.

GROWING NOTES

Torch lilies eventually form thick clumps of evergreen grass-like leaves which are dramatic in themselves and mix well in many styles of gardens. The plants thrive in most climates, except the tropics, and tolerate frost, exposed sites, strong wind, or coastal conditions. They require full sun all day and very well drained soil, but are tough once established. Mature clumps can be divided for propagation, but plants are very slow to recover their full glory.

The torch lilies inspire great displays in the garden—from spectacular drifts to dramatic clumps. Popular cultivars include those with pale yellow or green flowers.

PHLOMIS FRUTICOSA

JERUSALEM SAGE

Despite its common name, and the fact that it does belong to the same family of plants as mints and salvias, the Jerusalem sage has little herbal value, although the aromatic leaves can be used for tea. It is, instead, an outstanding ornamental, with large, wrinkly gray-green leaves (similar to sage) growing into a sprawling mound, 3 ft (1 m) in height or more, and wider, in ideal conditions. From late spring throughout summer, the plant produces upright stems bearing distinct whorls of hooded golden-yellow blooms. These are set in bunches along the stem and open gradually, to provide many weeks of unique flowers.

GROWING NOTES

Originating in the Mediterranean region, this evergreen perennial adapts to various climates, from warm to cool, but prefers those which resemble its natural habitat. The plants are best in full sun, and require very well drained soil. They also tolerate coastal conditions and frost, and will withstand long dry seasons once established. Cut back stems after flowering to keep the plants compact.

The distinct whorled arrangement of Jerusalem sage flowers creates a long and outstanding display in spring and summer.

RANUNCULUS ACRIS
BUTTERCUP

Unlike the flashy annuals of many colors, this perennial *Ranunculus* is known for its shining yellow flowers, giving rise to its common name, the buttercup. So often unfairly bypassed in the garden for being vernacular, or mistaken for weedy namesakes, the buttercup deserves greater credit in cultivation. The bright open-faced simplicity of the yellow flowers is pure charm. The plant, a low-growing clump of lobed leaves to about 2 ft (60 cm) in width and height, is fully frost hardy and undemanding in the garden. The double form has multi-petals which give the flowers a rounded appearance, and is officially *Ranunculus acris* 'Flore Pleno' but quaintly known as bachelor's buttons.

Shining buttercup flowers appear on top of fine wiry stems from late spring to early summer. They are especially charming in meadows and other wild gardens.

GROWING NOTES

Buttercups are meadow flowers of European marshlands and hence have a preference for moist soils and full sun in cool climates. They are, however, readily adaptable to cultivation and will equally thrive in warmer gardens if generously watered. Remove finished flower stems to tidy plants, and divide clumps every few years for propagation.

RUDBECKIA LACINIATA & CULTIVARS
YELLOW CONEFLOWER

The yellow coneflower *Rudbeckia laciniata* is one of the ornamental garden's most outstanding perennials, for both its striking flowers and towering form. Typical of the genus *Rudbeckia*, a small group of northern American wildflowers, the flower heads have tapered ray florets of gleaming yellow-gold and hard central cones of green, burgundy, or black. But these coneflowers are also the largest of their kind, growing into towering clumps 5–8 ft (1.5–2.5 m) in height. Only one other species is commonly grown, the annual *R. hirta*, or black-eyed Susan. However, many cultivars and hybrids of yellow coneflowers are available, including those with red-splashed ray petals, or semi-double and double flower heads, or with jet-black cones.

GROWING NOTES
The yellow coneflower grows in most climates except the tropics. The plants require full sun, well-drained soil and protection from strong wind. Remove old flower heads to promote new blooms, and cut back stems to ground level after flowering has ceased. Yellow coneflowers are easily propagated by seed or division of clumps.

Yellow coneflowers bloom in summer and fall; they are long-lasting in the garden or as cut flowers.

SEDUM SPECIES
STONECROP

Stonecrops form a large genus of succulents. Many species, including *Sedum adolphi* (above), are grown for their ornamental leaves as well as their flowers.

There are more than 200 species in this large genus of succulent plants, many of which are grown exclusively for their ornamental leaves, while others are cultivated for their starry five-petaled blooms. Most stonecrops, however, combine appealing flowers and cute foliage; for example, the yellow-flowering *Sedum rubrotinctum*, the jellybean plant, with shiny green leaves that turn red, yellow, and pink when conditions are dry or cold; the white-flowered *S. adolphi*, which has pale green leaves that take on peachy red-pink tones; and *S. spathulifolium*, with clusters of yellow flowers and minuscule gray-blue leaves in tiny rosettes.

Stonecrops are often featured in shallow pots, desert-style gardens, and rockeries, but there are also some *Sedum* species which suit flower borders: *S. spectabile* grows to 2 ft (60 cm) in height and has flat clusters of pink to red flowers; and

S. aizoon, a slightly smaller-growing species that has fleshy lance-shaped leaves and yellow starry flower clusters.

GROWING NOTES

All stonecrops, being succulent plants, are easy to grow and adaptable to most climates. Depending on the species, the plants may be tolerant of heavy frost (such as *S. spathulifolium*) or they may behave in a herbaceous manner during cold weather (like *S. spectabile*). Some are very successfully grown indoors. Most stonecrops prefer full sun, though light shade is tolerated by some species. In the garden or in containers, the plants require very well drained soil, with an open and coarse texture. Do not overwater: allow the soil to dry out before watering, and water plants only occasionally in winter. All stonecrops are easily propagated, either by division or from cuttings (leaf or stem).

The great variety of stonecrops ensures they suit many garden designs: *Sedum spectabile* (left) is easily placed in flower borders; *S. rubrotinctum* (above) is ideal for rockeries and pots.

SOLIDAGO CULTIVARS
GOLDENROD

The wild species of goldenrod, once widely considered to have healing properties, have been outlawed in many regions for their rather weedy habits of prolific seeding. Originating from woodland edges and rough fields, the two most common species, *Solidago canadensis*, from eastern North America, and *S. virgaurea*, from Europe, are extremely vigorous and prone to get out of control in the garden. There are, however, cultivars of both species which have perfected the ornamental value of these herbaceous perennials while controlling their invasive qualities. The cultivars tend to be compact-growing and less troublesome, but more floriferous, too, producing plumes of tiny flowers in clouds of yellow-gold throughout late summer.

The tiny flowers of goldenrod are borne in prolific sprays, creating a late summer cloud of yellow-gold.

GROWING NOTES

Even the cultivars of goldenrod are extremely adaptable to most garden climates, but they are especially vigorous in warmer areas. Plants will grow in full sun or part shade, and aren't fussy about soil. Whether growing from a rhizome or root crown, depending on the cultivar, the plants can be easily divided every few years.

ZANTEDESCHIA HYBRIDS
CALLA LILY

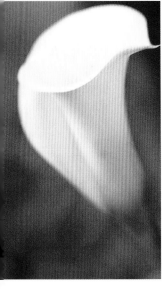

Calla lilies are created in a rich range of colors; the plants flower in late spring or early summer when grown in the garden.

The calla lily is a colorful invention. These highly desirable hybrids mostly derive from the golden calla (*Zantedeschia elliottiana*) and the pink calla (*Z. rehmannii*); and, unlike the oft-weedy arum lilies *Z. aethiopica* (see page 466), they form compact clumps usually no more than 1½ ft (45 cm) in height and rarely, if ever, get out of control. The calla's swirling spathes that surround the actual flower (the spadix) may be ruby-red, pink, orange, yellow, gold, or cream, and often in combinations of these decadent tones. Many also have silver-splashed leaves, adding to the visual feast.

GROWING NOTES

Callas are easily grown in gardens and pots in most climates from tropical to cool (in cold climates, they need conservatories). The plants are best in dappled sunlight (which also shows off the spotty leaves) or part shade, with morning sun only. They require shelter from strong wind and well-drained, enriched soil. The rhizomes eventually form small dense clumps and may be divided for propagation.

cool

The cool-colored flowers are like living jewels in the garden. All over the world, gardeners are drawn to these blooms—of deepest, darkest indigo to softest lilac to bright sky and azure. Cool colors are the most popular of flowers, and they complement many garden styles—literally, from the mountains to the sea—but their allure is itself a mystery.

Cool colors in the garden are alluring but also induce a sense of calm: here, the lilac spires of *Linaria purpurea* are a flowering feature. PREVIOUS PAGES: *Agapanthus orientalis*.

In the garden, cool colors are based on blue, a natural complement to green. Cool-colored flowers are eyecatching, but never clash; and, even when used in uplifting contrasts, such as with white, yellow, or red, they always seem serene. They can be gem-like in shade, but also dazzling under the sun. Cool colors can create an illusion of distance, but also evoke a sense of calm.

Many perennial flowers are famous for their cool colors, such as the delphinium and the bellflower. They are outstanding in designs, but also mingle amiably with other colors. RIGHT: *Hydrangea macrophylla*.

In this chapter, we celebrate the perennial flowers of purple and blue. Some of the blooms have become famous purely for these colors; others may include many hues in their flower range but are most well known for their cool. In nature and in the garden, blues and purples harmonize with pastels and neutrals: these chapters also contain inspiring flowers for cool-colored designs.

Cool colors are enriched when combined with pastels and neutral tones, and create an illusion of distance. FOLLOWING PAGES: The magical atmosphere of a design in cool colors is enhanced by the element of water.

AGAPANTHUS ORIENTALIS
AGAPANTHUS

The agapanthus is a great landscaper, effortless and effective. Flower clusters may each have more than a hundred blooms.

The agapanthus is one of the world's great landscapers. There is hardly a perennial more hardy or more reliable in design. And even though extensive plantings of these flowers have become a common feature in our cities, parks, and gardens, a great drift of agapanthus blue, or white, or both, remains a spectacular sight.

Agapanthus orientalis (syn. *A. praecox*) originates from South Africa's southern tip, but it has adapted to many climates, from hot and warm to temperate and quite cool. The plant forms a dense clump of strappy evergreen leaves and has thick sinewy roots, making it very resistant to drought and also to light frost. The flower clusters, often bearing more than a hundred blooms, appear on tall stems from late spring throughout summer, depending on the climate. The species has lilac-blue flowers, but the white variety is equally popular. There are also cultivars, some miniature in habit, with darker or paler blue flowers or double-petaled blooms.

Cultivars include dwarf varieties, forms with flowers in selected shades of blue, and the ever-popular all-white variation (below).

GROWING NOTES

Agapanthus will thrive in the toughest of garden conditions, while providing great visual impact. The plants can be used to stabilize soil on steep embankments, to line driveways and roads, or to create massive drifts of color. They can also be planted in pots, and will easily fill tubs, troughs, urns, and other large containers.

Agapanthus will grow in sun or shade, but flowering is reduced in heavy shade. The plants aren't fussy about soil, but well drained and enriched with organic matter is of course preferred. Regular watering helps new plants to establish, and produces the best growth and flowering of older plants; however, established agapanthus will also cope with drought. Clumps may be divided in late winter or early spring.

AJUGA REPTANS
BUGLE FLOWER

The bugle flower forms a low drift of deep and subtle colors: flower spires appear in spring or early summer.

In shaded places where it is often found, the bugle flower's dark and subtle colors come to life—deep oceanic greens and night-sky violet, blackened bronze and purple, tones rich but cool. An evergreen ground cover, it forms small rosettes of shiny leaf, growing no more than 6 in (15 cm) in height. The plants spread, by stolons, in a tightly packed low drift—ideal under trees, on banks, in pots and troughs, and to suppress weeds. The most common species of bugle flower, *Ajuga reptans*, with dark green leaves and deep violet blooms, can be invasive in ideal conditions; but its cultivars, especially those with purple, bronze, or variegated cream and pink leaves, are usually less vigorous.

GROWING NOTES

Bugle flowers will grow in most garden climates, but prefer moist well-drained soil. In warmer conditions, they require shade or dappled light under deciduous trees. In cool climates, they like more sun. The colors of the ornamental leaf cultivars, especially the variegated types, are also better in bright light situations.

CAMPANULA SPECIES
BELLFLOWER

M any kinds of plants masquerade under the banner of bellflower, from minute rockery plants and woodland ground covers sprinkled with starry blooms to tall meadow flowers with flamboyant spires. They originate from various habitats and all over the world: on mountain ranges in the northern hemisphere; in the fields and woodlands of Europe, Africa and Asia; and in rock crevices of the Mediterranean cliffs. All types of *Campanula*, however, have one common feature—the *campana*, or bell.

The characteristic shape of the bellflower is formed by a tubular corolla and five flared lobes. Depending on the degree of dilation, the flower can appear open and starry, like the Italian bellflower, *Campanula isophylla*, or pendent and thimble-shaped as in *C. rotundifolia*, the harebell. Most of the perennial bellflower species have blooms that are blue, purple, lilac, or white (though the annual or biennial Canterbury bell, *C. medium*, has cultivars with pink or violet flowers). Some of the trailing ground-covering types, like *C. poscharskyana*, have blooms along lax stems and flower profusely, and successively,

Perennial species of bellflowers include the upright-growing *Campanula persicifolia* (left), which has many cultivars, including those with white blooms.

The ground-covering species *Campanula portenschlagiana* (above) has flowers from spring to summer. *C. trachelium* (right) has tall stems of blooms that make excellent cut flowers.

for many months. The herbaceous, upright-growing species, such as the European and Asian wildflower *C. trachelium*, are more likely to form basal clumps and have tall, erect racemes of elegant bells.

GROWING NOTES

With about 300 species and numerous hybrids and cultivars, there are bellflowers for a wide range of garden conditions. Some, like the harebell, require full sun and cool to cold climates and will withstand below-freezing winter temperatures; while others, such as *C. poscharskyana*, vigorously adapt to much warmer regions and slight shade. Most prefer well-drained soil, and some can be grown in containers. Propagation methods vary depending on the species or cultivar, but dividing clumps or taking cuttings is easy and reliable.

CERATOSTIGMA WILLMOTTIANUM
CERATOSTIGMA

Covered in bright blue flowers throughout summer, and with deciduous leaves taking on autumnal burgundy tones, *Ceratostigma willmottianum* was a sure bet for success when it was introduced to Western gardeners about a century ago. A member of the plumbago family, it originates from China but was horticulturally established by British gardening personality of the time, Miss Ellen Ann Willmott, after whom the species is named. The plant has an open, low-growing, spreading shrub-like habit of small leaves that turn purple or red in the fall, often in tandem with the last flushes of flowers, creating a rare combination of seasonal colors.

Ceratostigma flowers from summer to fall. At the change of seasons, the blooms combine with the burgundy tones of the deciduous leaves.

GROWING NOTES

This species of ceratostigma will grow in most garden climates, except the hot tropics. It is also moderately frost hardy. Light, well-drained soils and sunny positions are best, but slight shade is preferred in warmer climates. Leave the old stems on the plant in winter (this protects the crown from frost), and prune back in spring.

CONVOLVULUS MAURITANICUS
MOROCCAN GLORY BIND

Moroccan glory bind flowers are typically misty mauve-blue, and only open on sunny days. The plants have a long flowering season, from spring to late fall.

From a large family of plants that includes morning glories, bindweeds, and moonflowers—all with the tell-tale trumpet-shaped blooms—the Moroccan glory bind is neither invasive nor temperamental, unlike many of its relatives. A low-growing trailing perennial with soft, small leaves and misty mauve to pale blue flowers, *Convolvulus mauritanicus* (sometimes known as *C. sabatius*) grows quickly but is compact and easy to contain. These plants are particularly attractive in ground-covering and cascading situations—spilling from hanging baskets or window boxes, or tumbling over low walls and alongside paths.

GROWING NOTES

Moroccan glory bind prefers tropical and warm climates, where it flowers throughout the year except in winter. In cooler regions, it grows well in sheltered microclimates, protected from frost. Full sun is required to produce dense growth and maximize flowers. These plants also need very well drained soil with a coarse structure. Once established, they are resistant to drought and trouble-free.

CORYDALIS SPECIES & CULTIVARS
CORYDALIS

Most types of corydalis flower in spring; and some will continue until early summer.

These highly desirable perennials have only recently, in the last few decades, been made widely available, but how quickly they have fallen into our favor. Mostly from Asia and Europe, the corydalis, with delicate, fern-like bright green leaves and flowers in clusters, has proven to be very adaptable in cultivation too. Not surprisingly, the species with blue flowers are particularly coveted in gardens, such as the Himalayan *Corydalis cashmeriana*, which has long curved spurs on narrow tubular flowers. There are also blue-flowering cultivars, like 'Blue Panda,' appearing on the market throughout the world, as well as a few pink and crimson forms. Also popular is *C. lutea*, a European species with yellow or white flowers.

GROWING NOTES

Most herbaceous perennial types of corydalis require full sun in cool climates, but some adapt to warmer gardens where they prefer dappled shade. The plants need well-drained soil and regular watering in the warm seasons. Some species will set seed, but cultivars should be divided (either by tuber offset or clump) for propagation.

CYNARA CARDUNCULUS
CARDOON

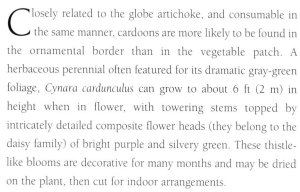

The flower heads of cardoon are long-lasting throughout summer and fall, and remain decorative as they age.

Closely related to the globe artichoke, and consumable in the same manner, cardoons are more likely to be found in the ornamental border than in the vegetable patch. A herbaceous perennial often featured for its dramatic gray-green foliage, *Cynara cardunculus* can grow to about 6 ft (2 m) in height when in flower, with towering stems topped by intricately detailed composite flower heads (they belong to the daisy family) of bright purple and silvery green. These thistle-like blooms are decorative for many months and may be dried on the plant, then cut for indoor arrangements.

GROWING NOTES

Cardoons can be grown in most garden climates, except the tropics. The plants require full sun all day and rich well-drained soil, with regular watering throughout the growing season. Cut back the plant to just above ground level when it dies off. Divide clumps or remove suckers in late winter for propagation; cardoons may be grown from seed but the plants vary in quality and are usually slow to flower.

DELPHINIUM SPECIES & CULTIVARS
DELPHINIUM

Delphinium flowers open one by one along the towering spire, in late spring or summer.

There are no words or even pictures that can capture the living color of delphinium flowers—you really have to be there. Which is, of course, why they are among the most desired of all flowers, perennial or otherwise, both in the garden and for the vase.

The eastern European meadow flower *Delphinium elatum* is the species for which the blue flower is best known, but there are also those with red or yellow blooms, all together contributing to the many cultivars of tantalizing colors. For hundreds of years, delphiniums have been hybridized and the results are intense purples, dreamy pinks or lilac, pristine whites with black velvet centers, double petals and semi-doubles, and of course the many immeasurable and indescribable blues.

GROWING NOTES

Apart from glorifying color, hybridization of these plants has also improved their hardiness. The modern delphiniums are designed for easy garden cultivation and a long flowering season. Most are herbaceous perennials in cool to cold climates, where they enjoy full sun and establish themselves in clumps, but there are also cultivars that grow as annuals or

Modern hybrids include the Pacific Series (opposite), short-lived perennials suitable for less than cool climates, but with the full range of flower colors.

biennials in more temperate gardens. None of the delphiniums, however, like warm, arid, or tropical conditions.

In the garden, to make the most of their uniqueness, delphiniums are best planted in dense drifts that indulge in one color or tone. Planted with other perennials, in mixed borders or cottage-style gardens, delphiniums provide height: in flower, they can reach at 3–6 ft (1–2 m) and some of the taller stems may need staking. The plants appreciate shelter from strong winds, attention to watering during spring and summer, and a rich soil enhanced by copious amounts of organic material. For indoor arrangements, cut the stems when nearly all the flowers are open.

DICHORISANDRA THYRSIFLORA
BLUE GINGER

The exotic flower spires and giant glossy leaves of blue ginger evoke its jungle origins; flowering lasts from summer to fall.

With spires of saturated flower color and giant, glossy leaves, dichorisandras evoke the richness of the southern Brazilian jungles from which they originate. These evergreen perennials can tower at more than 6 ft (2 m) in height in the tropics, but they usually grow only half as tall in cultivation (and slowly, too). The cane-like stems are produced from short rhizomes that gradually spread, and the plant eventually forms a dramatic clump. Its large leaves are held in informal whorls, a verdant backdrop for the deep purple-blue flower spikes in summer.

GROWING NOTES

Blue gingers prefer tropical or subtropical climates, but they will also grow in warm, frost-free gardens. The plants require shady conditions, protected from hot midday sun, such as in the dappled light of a canopy of trees or under a shaded pergola. The soil should be organically rich and well drained. Water the plants generously throughout the warmer seasons. To propagate, take stem cuttings in early spring or fall, or divide the clumps in late winter.

ECHINOPS SPECIES & CULTIVARS
GLOBE THISTLE

The globe thistle is a paragon of color and structure. Its spherical flower head is composed of hundreds of tiny starry florets (being a member of the daisy clan), in blues so bright they take on a metallic sheen. Each bloom is borne on a silvery stem, some species up to 6 ft (2 m) tall, and lasts for weeks, even retaining color when dried. Most frequently found in discerning gardens are the blue-flowering species, *Echinops bannaticus* and *E. ritro*, and their cultivars; as well as *E. sphaerocephalus*, a giant with mercurial silver-gray flowers.

GROWING NOTES

Globe thistles suit cool to warm climates, but require full sun and open aspects to perform best. The soil must be very well drained, but may be poor, rocky, or sandy. Herbaceous, with spiky, sharply divided leaves, the plants grow in basal clumps which may be divided for propagation (wear thick gloves when handling). Stems for drying should be cut before the flower head fully opens.

Under the open sky and backlit by the sun, the flower heads of *Echinops* become globes of glowing color and light.

ECHIUM FASTUOSUM
PRIDE OF MADEIRA

Hundreds of tiny flowers conspire to create the giant panicle which transforms the pride of Madeira into a garden spectacular. An evergreen perennial with a sprawling constitution, *Echium fastuosum* (syn. *E. candican*) can grow to 5 ft (1.5 m) in height and spreads much wider, but it is long-lived only in Mediterranean-type climates. The plant is multi-stemmed with whorls of large gray-green leaves, providing a silvery stage for the brilliant blue flowers. With each plant capable of producing many panicles, the pride of Madeira should never be confined to poky garden places. It thrives in open aspects and coastal conditions, where it can tower towards the sun.

GROWING NOTES

Although it prefers hot and warm climates, with dry summers, pride of Madeira will also grow in cool regions if protected from heavy frost. These plants must have full sun all day, excellent air circulation, and very well drained soil. They are particularly successful in dry, poor-quality, rocky, or sandy soils. Remove finished flower stems and, if required, trim plants during the growing season to keep them compact.

Echium fastuosum flowers from spring to early summer; it is also known as the tower of jewels.

FELICIA AMELLOIDES
KINGFISHER DAISY

Kingfisher daisies quickly form low mounds of fine leaf and bloom. The plants flower from spring through summer to fall.

Blue as the proverbial skies of its native South Africa, the kingfisher daisy is intensely hued and dazzling with color. It's the combination of complete opposites—electric blue ray florets around a starkly yellow center—that creates this energy. No other flower manages to make blue look so hot. And for so little effort. In suitable conditions, *Felicia amelloides* grows quickly into soft mounds of small rounded leaves—easily filling border edges, rockery pockets, or containers. There are cultivars which vary in flower color from pale lilac to purple, as well as those with larger-than-usual blooms.

GROWING NOTES

This evergreen perennial loves warm and hot climates, but also thrives in temperate and cool areas if protected from frost. It prefers full sun and very well drained soil. Trim off finished flower heads to prolong the season (use scissors or shears), and prune straggly plants in winter to keep them compact. The plants are less productive and tend to sprawl after a few years, but are easily propagated from cuttings.

GENTIANA ACAULIS
TRUMPET GENTIAN

This famous wildflower of European mountain ranges, from a genus of ancient herbs, and namesake of the unique color gentian blue, is quite rare in gardens—but not through lack of gardeners' wanting. The infrequency of trumpet gentians is simply due to their requirement for precise garden conditions: cool to cold and mountainous, reflecting their natural habitats. An evergreen perennial, the plant grows about 4 in (10 cm) in height, forming crowded rosettes of small, glossy green narrow leaves. It is the emblem of the Alpine Garden Society, being ideal for rockeries, raised beds, and alpine houses where the plant's cultivation needs may be matched and its spring flowers may be closely admired.

GROWING NOTES

Apart from a cool climate, *Gentiana acaulis* also requires full sun, protection from strong wind, and very well drained, gritty soil. While the plants enjoy plenty of moisture in summer, they need to be kept dry in winter. The species may be propagated by seed, but dividing plants or offsets in spring is easier and more reliable.

Gentiana acaulis is the doyen of the alpine garden; its spring flowers define the color gentian blue.

GERANIUM SPECIES & CULTIVARS
GERANIUM

Geranium flower colors span almost the entire spectrum. Among the most prized are the blue-flowering forms, such as *Geranium* x *magnificum* (right).

The naming of geraniums and pelargoniums has led to much confusion over the past two centuries, since it was officially recognized that, while they are closely related, the two plants are not the same. It all comes down to the flower. Doubles, hybrids and cultivars aside, the geranium's five petals are all the same in each flower; while two petals in the pelargonium's flower differ from the other three (see page 96).

The geranium goes back at least as far as the ancient Greeks, who named it *geranion*, cranesbill, alluding to the shape of its seed pod. There are more than 300 species of *Geranium*, and these have produced a multitude of hybrids and cultivars. Their flower colors span almost the entire spectrum—from dark velvety crimson and rosy pink to pure purples and true blues, as well as opalescent white, sometimes with just a hint of color or finely striped.

Most geraniums are perennial, with lobed, deeply divided, or near-feathery leaves that form compact rounded clumps. Some of the low-growing types suit rockeries, edging, ground cover, and containers such as hanging baskets and window boxes. Others are taller, mixing well with perennials and also shrubs, in meadow plantings and flower borders.

All the garden geraniums have a long flowering season. *Geranium* x *cantabrigiense* 'Biokovo' (opposite) is a low-growing hybrid with lobed leaves and pale pink flowers.

GROWING NOTES

Depending on the type, geraniums will grow in most garden climates, though some do prefer cool conditions. They generally like full sun, but light shade is appreciated in warmer climates. The plants require very well drained soil that is not too acidic. Most species will grow easily from seed, but the resulting plants can vary; taking cuttings or dividing plants is more reliable, and the only way of propagating hybrids and cultivars. Remove the finished flowers to prolong the season and to keep plants compact.

Heliotropes flower from spring throughout summer; the plants are cloaked in mauve-purple clusters and have a sweet vanilla aroma.

HELIOTROPIUM ARBORESCENS
HELIOTROPE

Often known as cherry pie, the heliotrope in flower is cloaked in mauve-purple clusters and a strong vanilla aroma, creating swathes of color as well as fragrance. Evergreens from South America, the plants have soft-stemmed, bushy shrub-like habits, and usually grow about 2 ft (60 cm) in height but spread much wider—sensational features in full bloom. Only one species, *Heliotropium arborescens*, is commonly grown but includes popular cultivars such as 'Lord Roberts,' with dark purple-green leaves and violet flowers, and 'Aureum,' with bright yellow-green leaves and pale lilac blooms.

GROWING NOTES
Heliotropes are suitable only for tropical to temperate gardens, being intolerant of even the lightest frost. The plants prefer full sun and shelter from strong wind, but will also grow in part shade. They require well-drained soil, preferably enriched with organic material, and regular deep watering in warm weather. Cuttings are easily struck—the plants reach maturity within a few years, and can be quite long-lived.

KNAUTIA SPECIES
KNAUTIA

The genus *Knautia*, a small group of summer-flowering herbaceous perennials, has only recently made the break from its close relation the scabiosa or pincushion flower (*Scabiosa* species). In fact, knautias are still frequently classified as *Scabiosa*, and share its common names. Only two species of knautia are cultivated in gardens: the crimson-flowered *Knautia macedonica* (syn. *Scabiosa rumelica*); and *K. arvensis*, with blooms of lilac-blue. Both these knautias have soft, slightly furry leaves that grow in basal clumps, and rounded flower heads of fine florets on lofty stems in summer.

GROWING NOTES

Knautias (and scabiosas) grow in most climates, except the tropics, and they will also withstand frost. They require full sun and well-drained soil; slight shade is tolerated but flowering can be compromised. Flower stems should be staked for blooms to be best displayed; remove finished flowers to encourage further flushes. Take basal cuttings or divide offsets from clumps in early spring for propagation.

Knautias are closely related to scabiosas, but only two species are commonly grown. *Knautia arvensis* has summer flower heads of lilac-blue.

LIMONIUM LATIFOLIUM
SEA LAVENDER

Sea lavender flowers from spring to summer; the colorful clusters last for many months in the garden, and even longer when the stems are cut and dried.

This meadow wildflower of south-eastern and central Europe, a perennial form of statice, is much favored by flower arrangers for its abundant panicles of papery "everlasting" blooms. It's actually the calyces which are colorful—usually lavender-blue, but also pink or violet—and long-lasting; the flowers being small, white, and short-lived. In the garden, too, sea lavender gives great value. An evergreen with broad rounded leaves in basal clumps, it happily grows in dry garden beds and hostile rocky places but also mixes well in many kinds of borders. The flower stems are flattened and strong, up to 2 ft (60 cm) in length, and ideal for cutting.

GROWING NOTES

Limonium latifolium grows in most warm to cool climates, but is unsuitable for the tropics and regions with high humidity or rainfall in summer. The plants will withstand frost, exposure to wind, as well as coastal conditions; once established, they are also fairly tolerant of drought. They require full sun and very well drained soil. Propagate from freshly ripened seed, or from root cuttings in early spring. Cutting flower stems helps to keep the plants compact.

LITHODORA DIFFUSA
BLUE LITHODORA

The pure royal blue flowers of lithodora are highly regarded among lovers of cool color, but this prostrate perennial is also popular as a compact ground cover or small cascade. Blue lithodora has loosely trailing, fine evergreen foliage which suits rockeries and stone gardens, but also looks charming when spilling over low walls or the edges of raised beds. Once classified as *Lithospermum* (hence any confusion over its name), *Lithodora diffusa* originates in southern and western Europe and Morocco. A few cultivars exist, either with larger flowers or in a slightly different hue.

GROWING NOTES

Blue lithodora prefers cool to cold climates and must have full sun and very well drained, acidic soils. It will also grow in cooler parts of more temperate regions, but not in areas of high summer rainfall or humidity. Poorly drained soil and waterlogging will kill the plants; however, they are perfect for raised conditions such as rockeries. Propagate from cuttings in spring or by seed sown in the fall.

Blue lithodora flowers profusely throughout spring. Its trailing form is ideal for rockeries and stone gardens.

MECONOPSIS BETONICIFOLIA
HIMALAYAN BLUE POPPY

Setting a benchmark
in flower color, the
Himalayan blue poppy
Meconopsis betonicifolia.

When this plant first came to the gardening public's attention less than a century ago, in 1927 in the botanical parks of Glasgow, it redefined blue. It gave the color a new form of expression as a flower.

There is no blue like the *Meconopsis betonicifolia* and to grow and flower the Himalayan blue poppy has become a horticultural epiphany. There are gardeners who have made pilgrimages to its Tibetan homelands to see it growing in its natural state, and others who have moved to cooler climes for the opportunity to grow it at home. For many followers of garden blues, it is the holy grail of flowers.

Although this perennial has only become widely available in the past decade or so, the Himalayan blue poppy is already

Himalayan blue poppies prefer conditions that replicate their cool mountainous homelands. They can flower from late spring throughout summer.

well-established as a garden favorite. *M. betonicifolia* has been the most popular, and reliable, of the blue poppies; however, other species with equally astounding flowers, also from China and the Himalayas, are becoming better known. The blue poppies have one European relative—*M. cambrica*, the yellow-flowered Welsh poppy.

GROWING NOTES

To be successful in the garden, blue poppies require similar conditions to their native habitats: in general, these are cool, cold or mountainous climates and very fertile, humus-rich, moist, and acidic soil. The plants may survive poor or limey soil or slightly warmer conditions, but the flowers will be of a lesser blue. Even in ideal growing conditions, the blue poppy is likely to be a short-lived perennial, flowering only after its first year. It is mostly grown from seed sown in the fall, or from root crowns planted in winter.

NEPETA X *FAASSENII*
CATMINT

The mauve-flowered catmint is a human invention. A hybrid of two species, *Nepeta* x *faassenii* is popular with gardeners, while felines prefer the white-flowered species *N. cataria* (a catmint also used herbally). The hybrid catmint is, of course, easy to grow, with aromatic, soft gray-green leaves in long-lived bushy clumps. The flowers appear on loose spikes and in massed plantings they form a haze of color, but catmint also mixes well with other plants: in rockeries or containers (such as hanging baskets and window boxes), as edging, among roses (where they have found a special niche), and in herb gardens or cottage borders.

Hybrid catmints produce many flowers throughout spring and summer; in massed plantings, they form a mauve-blue haze.

GROWING NOTES

Catmints thrive in most garden climates, except the tropics, but do prefer hot dry summers and cool to cold winters. Full sun is best, but plants also grow in part shade. A well-drained soil, though not necessarily rich, is essential; catmints are tough but intolerant of overwatering or poorly drained soil. They are easily propagated from suckers or cuttings.

PLATYCODON GRANDIFLORUS
BALLOON FLOWER

A natural rarity, the balloon flower belongs to a genus, *Platycodon*, of only one species. Originating from Japan and China, these herbaceous perennials are distinguished by their balloon-like flower buds that open into flared bells of chalk white, pastel pink, or shades of purple or blue. Among the many named cultivars, there are also those with semi-double or double blooms, as well as dwarf forms. The plants generally grow to about 2 ft (60 cm) in height in cultivation, and spread slowly into compact clumps. The dwarf forms may be only half as tall, but their flowers are just as uniquely spectacular as the species.

Botanically unique, balloon flowers bloom throughout summer. They are long-lasting as cut flowers.

GROWING NOTES
Balloon flowers prefer cool to cold climates, but they can also be grown in some cooler areas of temperate regions. The plants require full sun or lightly dappled shade, with protection from the hot sun in warmer gardens. Soil should be organically rich, moist and well-drained; the plants dislike soggy conditions. Remove finished flower stems to prolong blooming, and cut plants to ground level when foliage dies off.

PLECTRANTHUS SACCATUS
SPUR FLOWER

The spur flower belongs to a large genus of tropical and subtropical herbs, *Plectranthus*, which is part of the mint family, but also closely related to coleus. Like many of its relatives, *P. saccatus* has aromatic leaves and square stems; however, this evergreen perennial is more often grown for its flowers than its foliage. These are proportionately large (compared to other mints), prettily colored in tones of pale lilac-blue, and produced over a long period from midsummer and into fall. In the garden, this spur flower can be used as a tall fragrant ground cover or in containers; it can also be grown as an indoors plant.

Spur flowers, including *Plectranthus australis* (above) and *P. saccatus* (right), thrive in shady gardens, but they also grow indoors.

GROWING NOTES

Spur flowers prefer warm and tropical climates, but they will adapt to cool frost-free areas or indoor cultivation in pots. They require light shade or morning sun only, with shelter from strong wind, and regular watering. After several years, the plants can become straggly and unproductive, but are easily propagated from cuttings or rooted stems which spread out from the clump.

POLEMONIUM CAERULEUM
JACOB'S LADDER

Native to the grasslands and rocky meadows of northern and central Europe and northern Asia, these perennials were once cultivated as herbs (though for rather doubtful purposes) but are now best known as favorites of the cottage garden. *Polemonium caeruleum* is easily recognized by the paired arrangement of its leaves on long upright stems, giving this plant its common name, a biblical reference to Jacob's ladder to heaven. It has tall racemes of lavender-blue flowers with yellow stamens, but cultivated forms may have blooms of dark sky blue or white. Though the leaves may appear delicate and ferny, these plants grow into large dense clumps that are outstanding massed or in mixed borders or containers.

Jacob's ladder flowers from spring to summer in cool climates; the plant's common name refers to the paired arrangement of its leaves.

GROWING NOTES

Jacob's ladder prefers cool climates, where it is herbaceous and likes full sun. In more temperate areas, it tends to be evergreen and requires part shade. The plants grow from creeping rhizomes, and clumps may be divided in early spring, but the species also seeds freely in suitable conditions (if required, remove just-finished flowers to prevent seeds from setting).

PONTEDERIA CORDATA
PICKEREL RUSH

The lucent colors and fluid form of the pickerel rush reveals its aquatic nature. Its large heart-shaped leaves on tall stems have rippling curves and are often marked with sweeping lines in shades of watery green. The flowers, borne on short spikes in spathe-like style, may be deep purple or bright sea blue. From eastern North America, this perennial is often featured in water gardens, at the edges of ponds, or in shallow pools, but the plants are very adaptable and will also grow in marginal conditions, wet garden soils, and water-holding containers such as wine barrels, bathtubs, and troughs. Unlike other aquatics growing from thick rhizomes that can become invasive, the pickerel rush slowly forms dense clumps that won't get out of hand.

Each flower spire of pickerel rush lasts for many weeks, and the plants may bloom for a long period from spring throughout summer into fall.

GROWING NOTES
Adaptable to climates from tropical to freezing cold, these evergreen perennials only become herbaceous with frost. The plants are best in full sun, but in hot climates they prefer part shade. Generously water plants in garden beds or containers in spring and summer, and keep the soil constantly moist.

PULMONARIA SPECIES & CULTIVARS
LUNGWORT

The tubular flowers of lungwort start to appear in winter or early spring; most *Pulmonaria* have silvery-spotted foliage.

Once cultivated for its medicinal qualities, based on the dubious assumption that plants resembled the ailing body parts they could cure, the lungwort retains this remedial association through its botanical and common names. These days, however, this European perennial is better valued for its ornamental appearance: shapely ovate leaves, often spotted pale silvery green, growing in low spreading clumps which produce many upright stems of tubular flowers. Though mostly in hues of rich royal blue, the blooms may also open pink and mature to deep violet. Shade-lovers by nature, lungworts are often used as ground cover under trees, between shrubs, and at the front of shady borders, where dappled light enhances their appeal.

GROWING NOTES

Suitable for cool climates only, these herbaceous plants prefer light shade and need protection from any strong sun. They require an organically enriched soil that is kept constantly moist throughout the growing season. Species can be grown from seed, but division of clumps is necessary for cultivars.

PULSATILLA VULGARIS
PASQUE FLOWER

Traditionally one of the first wildflowers to appear in spring, in its cold native habitat of northern Europe, the pasque flower's timeliness accounts for much of its appeal. The plants stir late in winter, long before other herbaceous perennials awake, and, often before their leaves are produced, they'll start to bloom—rich purple flowers covered in silky hairs that defy the cold and look sugar-coated in frost. Early, too, the leaves unfurl, fresh green and finely divided; they form a low feathery background for the spring flowers which are followed by long-lasting fluffy seed heads.

Pasque flowers start blooming in late winter, continuing throughout spring. The plants form feathery drifts well suited to rockeries and the front of borders.

GROWING NOTES

Pasque flowers prefer full sun in cool to cold climates, but will also adapt to temperate regions with frosty winters and low summer humidity (in warmer gardens, they appreciate part shade). The plants require well-drained, organically rich soil, and regular watering in spring and summer. To propagate, divide clumps during dormancy. Tactile as the whole plant seems, all parts can be irritating to handle and gardeners with sensitive skin should wear gloves.

ROSMARINUS OFFICINALIS
ROSEMARY

A king among herbs and in culinary circles, rosemary also has myriad uses in the ornamental garden. Naturally, it is a star attraction of herb knots, potagers, and parterres, but this evergreen perennial can also be grown as a hedge (clipped or informal), or in mixed borders, rockeries, and containers; the prostrate form of rosemary can even be used as a trailing type of ground cover. Planted along paths, beside steps, or around paving, its aromatic qualities can be appreciated every time you pass. In recent times, commercial cultivators of rosemary have concentrated more on its flowers, so that these plants now bring a wealth of color to the garden, too.

Most wild types of rosemary have lilac-blue spring flowers, but there are also cultivars with white or pale pink blooms, as well as trailing forms.

GROWING NOTES

Mediterranean in origin, rosemary prefers similar climates of dry, hot summers and cool to cold winters; however, it adapts to most garden regions, except the tropics. The plants are best in full sun all day, and must have very well drained soil. They will withstand coastal conditions and, once established, periods of drought. Rosemary is easily propagated by taking semi-hardwood cuttings.

SALVIA SPECIES & CULTIVARS
SAGE

Where would we be without sage? Even in medieval times (when such things were first recorded), the reputation of this herb was commonplace. It flavors our food, scents our homes and heals our bodies and sometimes even our souls. In the garden, sage is near sacred, representing a holy trio of foliage, fragrance, and flower, and many gardeners have found that one *Salvia* or two can lead to a collection.

There are more than 700 species of *Salvia*, the most famous of which is *Salvia officinalis*, the culinary sage, a perennial with infinitely valuable gray-green leaves and (less useful) pale purple flowers. Also well known are the annual border salvias, *S. splendens* and derivatives, with blazing red-toned blooms.

The perennial sages are usually herbaceous, though they may be evergreen in warm climates. The plants tend to grow in

The Mexican sage, *Salvia leucantha* (above), is a fall-flowering species, and large and sprawling in habit. 'Russian Blue' (left) is a cultivar of *S. farinacea*.

The mealy cup sage, *Salvia farinacea* (above), though short-lived, has cultivars with violet flowers as well as white. A favorite among favorites is *S. patens* (right), a tall grower with slender stems of flowers.

dense clumps, medium to tall in height, and some spread vigorously by underground stems. Most of the species have flowers that are based on purple, white, or blue, for which they are much desired. However, cultivars and hybrids also extend the color range to include cream, mauve, pink, and pale yellow. (Enter the collection!)

GROWING NOTES

Perennial salvias are generally easy to grow in climates from warm to cool. (In tropical areas, annual types are usually more suitable.) Most like full sun all day, but some will tolerate part shade, especially in warmer gardens. The plants require well-drained soil, though not necessarily rich. Once established, they are very resistant to drought, though occasional watering will promote growth and flowers. While species will grow from seed, cultivars and hybrids should be propagated from cuttings or divided. Remove finished flowers or cut back plants in early winter to keep them prolific and tidy.

SCAEVOLA SPECIES
FAN FLOWER

The distinct, five-petal fan arrangement of these flowers, produced in profusion, and the plant's adaptability to garden cultivation, have ensured a worldwide following for these mostly Australian perennials. Despite their demure appearance, though, fan flowers are tough: in their native habitats they often withstand coastal conditions and drought, stabilizing sand dunes and colonizing windswept cliffs. In the garden, fan flowers thrive as ground covers, in rockeries, or trailing over low banks, and in containers, especially hanging baskets and window boxes. The most commonly grown species are *Scaevola aemula*, the fairy fan flower, usually with blue or purple flowers; and *S. albida*, with pale blue, lilac, pink, or white blooms. Hybrids and cultivars with improved flowers and growing habits are increasingly available.

Fan flowers have a long season of blooms, from spring through summer and sometimes into fall as well.

GROWING NOTES
Fan flowers will grow in many garden climates, from cool to subtropical. They prefer full sun to light shade (heavy shade produces sparse and weak plants), and also require a very well drained soil. Water the plants regularly during dry seasons to ensure strong growth and flowering. Avoid using fertilizers with a high phosphorus content.

TRADESCANTIA VIRGINIANA
TRINITY FLOWER

A lso known as spiderwort or widow's tears, the trinity flower belongs to a large genus of perennials from northern and South America. Unlike its weedy cousin, a cursed invader of warmer climates, the wandering jew (*Tradescantia albiflora*), the trinity flower is highly ornamental and very well behaved. The plants have a spreading, but not invasive, habit of multi-stems and lax ribbon-like leaves, informally covering shaded garden areas such as between shrubs and under trees. They have a long flowering season, from spring through summer, although each bloom lasts only one day. Several cultivars are available, and these may have rich purple, lilac, mauve-pink, or white flowers.

Each bloom of the trinity flower lasts only one day, but there are many on the plant at once and more buds on the way.

GROWING NOTES

An adaptable perennial, the trinity flower is herbaceous in cooler climates, but semi-evergreen in warmer regions (it is not suitable for tropical areas). The plants prefer dappled shade, but will tolerate some morning sun, and require humus-rich well-drained soil. They are easily propagated by division of clumps in winter.

VERONICA SPECIES & CULTIVARS
SPEEDWELL

Perennial speedwells include prostrate species as well as upright-growing forms; *Veronica longifolia* usually has blue flowers but 'Alba' (right) is also a popular choice in cool-colored gardens.

The best known speedwells are usually found in flower borders, where their towering, tapering spires provide dramatic accents in purple, white, or blue. These include *Veronica longifolia* and its white-flowered cultivar 'Alba,' and *V. spicata*, with flowers that may be blue or lilac-pink. There are, however, also many prostrate perennial species, much suited to rockeries, alpine borders, and ground cover, such as *V. prostrata*, a low-growing, mat-forming species, with bright blue or purple blooms, and *V. cinerea*, which has gray-green leaves and white-centered flowers.

GROWING NOTES

Most of the perennial speedwells are herbaceous, and prefer cool climates. They can adapt to warm regions but not tropical, and some will also grow in shade. The prostrate, rockery types, especially the alpine species, generally like colder conditions and are very tolerant of frost. Many of the species are easily propagated from seed, but cuttings can also be taken during the growing season.

VINCA MINOR
PERIWINKLE

The periwinkle is one of the garden's most familiar ground covers. An evergreen, it is capable of densely carpeting even the most difficult situations—directly under trees, steep soil embankments, shaded rooftops, and window boxes—with trailing stems that can send out roots at every node. The flowers appear in spring: simple five-petal formations in gentlest lilac-blue. Cultivars of *Vinca minor* have a tonal range of flowers from dark blue and soft purple to palest lilac or all-white; however, there are also those with double-petaled blooms or brightly variegated leaves.

The gentle hues of the periwinkle flower are best in shaded conditions. The variegated form (right) provides foliage color all year round.

GROWING NOTES

Periwinkles may thrive in most climates except extremely hot or cold. In ideal conditions, such as moist gardens, *V. minor* can spread very quickly (though it's not as invasive as its close relative, *V. major*). Regular watering helps new plants to establish, while older periwinkles will benefit from occasional tip-pruning to keep their low-growing habits dense and lush.

VIOLA SPECIES & CULTIVARS
VIOLET

The flower of the sweet violet, *Viola odorata*, is a timeless favorite of poets, lovers, and gardeners.

The violet transcends the garden. It has long surpassed its status of mere flower and become a legend, daring to rival even the rose for romanticism. Cultivated in ancient gardens, medicinally valued by the Classical Greeks, grown in medieval monasteries, and the timeless favorite of artists, poets, and lovers (including the Emperor Napoleon Bonaparte, who, during his exile, is purported to have proclaimed the famous words "I will return with the violets in spring"), the violet has made quite an impact for a flower often described as humble or shy.

There are about 500 species of *Viola* and these are commonly divided into two groups: the pansies, with colorful flattened flowers; and the violets, which have more concave blooms that are most often purple. While the pansies (including heartsease and tricolors) are usually annual, the violets are generally perennial and often have creeping, ground-covering habits. *V. odorata*, the sweet violet, remains the best known, and its hybrid offspring and cultivars are many. These include the

Perennial violets, such as *Viola hederacea* (opposite), may be grown as ground covers beneath trees and in shade, but they will need some sunlight to flower well.

Parma violets, a group with double-petaled blooms and ambrosial fragrance, which had a popularity peak in Victorian times and are highly desirable once again.

GROWING NOTES

Most perennial violets are very easy to grow, and many species are adaptable (some can even be invasive). The sweet violet and its cultivars prefer cool climates but also grow in cooler parts of warm gardens. Violets do like shade or dappled light, being mostly woodland plants; however, they will need some sunlight to flower. In cool climates, they can be grown in full sun. Most species will readily self-seed, but all violets are easily divided and the cultivars and hybrids should only be propagated in this way.

lavender

In the world of cultivated plants, lavender stands alone. It's not like other iconic flowers, such as orchid or rose, that are grown on vast commercial scales. Nor is it like other harvested herbs, as it is rarely used for culinary purposes. Lavender is unique, and it is the plant's fragrance which has made it so.

The range of lavenders

for gardens includes the

fern-leaf types (top left);

Lavandula angustifolia (top

right); and *L. stoechas*

(bottom left and right).

Since Roman times, and no doubt before, we have used lavender to scent our bodies and our homes; to cleanse (its botanical name comes from the Latin, *lavare*, to wash) and antiseptize; and to heal—many of lavender's remedial properties have recently been proven in university tests, finding in science what all herbalists (and most gardeners) have always known.

Lavender has been planted in the garden ever since we had gardens in many cultures. Though now more ornamental than herbal, the lavenders are indisputable favorites. And many gardeners will agree with the lavender-holics—you simply can't have too many.

There are only about 30 species in the genus *Lavandula*, most originating around the Mediterranean area, from which only a handful are commonly grown. Their oft-used common names, such as French, Italian or Spanish, are misleading and even the experts in such matters can't agree. For example, *L. dentata*, the so-called French lavender, is actually from Spain. And English lavender is a misnomer, because *L. angustifolia* (syn. *L. spica*, syn. *L. officinalis*), the common lavender, was introduced to the British Isles (and many other places) by the Romans on their imperial sojourns.

Lavender-lined pathways invite with fragrant foliage and flower (these are nearing full bloom). Depending on the plant type, lavenders may flower from late winter through spring, or from spring through summer.

These species are joined in the garden by few others, including *Lavandula lanata*, the woolly lavender, with its furry leaves and stems; and *L. viridis*, the green lavender, which has unusual scented foliage and yellow-green flowers. Another group is known as the fern-leaf lavenders, such as *L. canariensis* and *L. multifida*, with their lacy foliage.

Of course, many lavender hybrids and cultivars abound, including those with flowers from white through all the shades of famous purple-blue to pink and even near-red. Their forms can vary, too, and some of the stoechas section (as they are formally known) feature flower heads topped with enlarged bracts or "ears." And probably the most widely grown of all lavenders is a hybrid—*Lavandula* x *intermedia* (the offspring of *L. dentata* and *L. latifolia*) has many cultivars of its own, and is the doyen of perfumery.

If you love lavender, it's worth shopping around. Many of its most exciting cultivars aren't found at the local chainstore, and while discerning garden centers will often stock something out-of-the-ordinary, it's the range available through specialist nurseries that will astound. The really good lavender growers will also supply their plants by mail-order (so you can easily extend your collection).

Ever popular with gardeners are the stoechas type (top and bottom left), with flowers topped by upward-sweeping bracts or "ears," and *Lavandula dentata* (top and bottom right).

A drift of lavender is a highlight of any garden. *Lavandula angustifolia* has a wide range of flower colors from darkest violet to pure white.

GROWING NOTES

Apart from any scent-related value, lavender is a great garden plant. Evergreen and dense with fine silvery-gray toned foliage, lavenders can be grown in borders, in drifts of their own, or mixed with other plants; but also in hedges, clipped as they once were in the early days of knot gardens and parterres, or informal and free-form. The plants thrive in pots, and are always enjoyed when placed beside pathways and doors.

All lavenders need full sun and an open aspect. The soil must be very well drained, preferably coarse or sandy, and slightly limey is ideal. The plants will grow in climates from warm to cold, but prefer conditions which are similar to their Mediterranean origins (cold, wet winters and hot, dry summers). They struggle in humidity. Water regularly to establish the plants, after which they are tolerant of dry spells. Removing flower stems, either newly opened for the vase or when finished, will prolong the season of blooms and tidy up the plants. Light tip-pruning also helps to maintain a compact shape. While plants can have long lives, they are often replaced after a few years when their productivity has waned. Lavender is very easily propagated from cuttings, but note that some of the named cultivars are protected by horticultural trademarks.

pastel

Pastels are the romantics of the garden. These are the sentimental tones, the whispers of colors, and the gentle hues of dawn and dusk. Pastels and flowers are synonymous—they share the same kind of beauty, speak the same language, and strike the same chord. In the garden, pastel designs are favored because they are colorful but so easy to live with too.

Pastel colors brightly and gently bring the garden to life, but they also seduce the eye and diffuse the boundaries of garden space. PREVIOUS PAGES: A pastel cultivar of tuberous begonia, *Begonia* x *tuberhybrida*.

Pastels are simply paler versions of colors, tempered by degrees of white, and, depending on their undertone, they too can be hot, cool or warm. Pastel-colored flowers mixed together have a reputation for creating harmony and dreamy gardenscapes, however, these pale colors can also be used in contrasts or as highlights. Pastels enliven gardens, but are never too bold.

Many of the flowering perennials include pale colors in their range of blooms, so there is an inspiring choice of plants which can be included in pastel garden designs. RIGHT: Polyantha rose, 'The Fairy.'

Pastel-colored flowers are easy to include in designs, and are plentiful as well. Many of the other perennial flowers in this book have pastel counterparts—these may be natural variations, but can be cultivated by gardeners, too. This chapter features flowers that are known for their pale beauty, but also some plants with a wide color range of which the pastels are among the most popular.

Pastels are among the most light-reflective of garden colors; they will blend with white but also with stronger tones. FOLLOWING PAGES: A pastel-colored garden of annuals and perennials, with warm undertones.

ACHILLEA SPECIES & CULTIVARS
YARROW

The floriferous beauties of *Achillea* which are grown in gardens today bear little resemblance to their wildflower ancestors. Nor do they look like the herb that was supposedly used by the Greek hero Achilles to treat his wounds (the legend from which the genus gets its botanical name).

The modern yarrow has come a long way. It is cultivated, vividly colored and less likely to become a weed. It is hailed as one of the most rewarding of flowering perennials—easy to grow and adaptable to many garden styles and situations, from meadows to pots; featuring feathery drifts of ferny foliage and flower heads, for months in summer and early fall, which cut well for arrangements, too.

Many of these modern yarrows, also commonly known as milfoil, are simply tried-and-trusted cultivars preferred over the wild forms, like *Achillea ptarmica* 'The Pearl,' which has larger-than-normal white blooms. Others may be hybrids, such as *A.* 'Moonshine,' which has bright yellow flower heads or *A.* 'Terracotta,' with blooms of earthy-orange tones. With some varieties, the colors change as the flower heads age, for

Yarrows planted in drifts are reminiscent of their wildflower ancestors, and create a spectacle of color throughout summer and early fall.

The ornamental yarrow features hundreds of tiny blooms composed in flower heads; the flowers of some cultivars change color as they age.

example from crimson to blushing pink, or from deep apricot to cream, creating an enchanting spectacle of hues.

GROWING NOTES

The ornamental forms of yarrow will thrive in most climates, except the tropics. The plants flower best in full sun all day, but will tolerate shade for a few hours. They prefer a well-drained soil, though they aren't fussy. Regular watering in spring promotes new growth, but once established the plants will withstand drought. Removing finished flower stems prolongs the season, as will cutting stems for the vase (as soon as the flower heads open). Clumps are easily divided for propagation.

ARGYRANTHEMUM FRUTESCENS
MARGUERITE DAISY

Marguerite daisies were originally only white or yellow but their colors now include many shades of pink, as well as single and double flower heads.

The daisy is the king of flowers. There are more than 20,000 species in the family (variously known as Compositae or Asteraceae) making it the most numerous of flowering plants. Daisies are everywhere. And all are distinguished by one common feature: a composite bloom.

Every daisy flower is actually hundreds, sometimes thousands, of flowers—a flower head. In most daisies, the outer circle of ray florets has brightly colored petals, while the inner bunch of tiny tube florets is usually yellow and tightly packed in a central disc. Within the family the theme may vary slightly but the composition is always the same.

The marguerite daisy has become one of the family's archetypes. Like many in the family, the marguerite has suffered name change after name change and is still often classified as *Chrysanthemum frutescens* (though the true chrysanthemums have long since broken away on their own).

For very little effort, the marguerite daisies provide spectacular sweeps of color for months. The plants are also easily grown in pots.

The marguerite is often referred to as the daisy bush. An evergreen perennial with divided, aromatic leaves, the plant grows into a mounded shrub about 3 ft (1 m) in size. Its flower heads, white, yellow, or pink, blanket the plants for months throughout spring and summer. Often used in expansive sweeps or in containers, the marguerite is, of course, a definitive daisy of cottage gardens and flower borders.

GROWING NOTES

Marguerite daisies grow in any climate. The plants are best in full sun all day, and prefer well-drained soil. Regular watering and an occasional feed will greatly improve growth and flowering. Plants can be short-lived, or less productive as they mature, but are very easily propagated by cuttings. Remove finished flower heads to ensure a long and prolific season.

ARMERIA MARITIMA
THRIFT

Thrift produces masses of flowers in spring and summer. The flower heads are very long-lasting in arrangements, either fresh or dried.

Although it is sometimes called sea pink, thrift is known as an evergreen perennial that thrives, and flowers profusely, on limited resources. Originating as it often does on cliff tops, mountains, and rugged coastlines around the Mediterranean and in northern Europe, thrift can handle the toughest of garden conditions—including rockeries, salt spray, stone walls, frost, drought, or poor soil. The plant's neat habit of grassy mounds, up to about 5 in (12 cm) in height, creates easy displays in flower borders, edgings, and containers, and it can also be used as ground cover. The flower heads, produced on long stems in masses throughout spring and summer, may be any shade of pink from tinted white to near red.

GROWING NOTES

Thrift suits almost any garden climate, except the tropics. The plants require full sun all day and very well drained, light soil: they rot in heavy soil or if overwatered. Clumps may be divided to propagate. Removing the finished flower stems will greatly prolong the season.

ASTILBE HYBRIDS
ASTILBE

Though their feathery plumes of thousands of tiny star-shaped flowers, in red, white, pink, or mauve, are outstanding in late spring and throughout summer, astilbes also have other seasonal attractions. These herbaceous perennials have compound leaflets that grow into dense clumps about 1 ft (30 cm) in height, and in some cultivars the new foliage has bronze or coppery-red tones. The flowers, while most ornamental when fully colored in summer, remain densely packed on the panicles throughout the fall, fading to soft brown. Dried and left on the plants, the plumes are a decorative feature of winter as well.

GROWING NOTES
Astilbes are best in cool climates, although they will grow in cooler parts of warmer areas. They love rich moist soil and can be planted in marginal areas, such as around ponds. The plants suit light shade, but in cool and cold climates they prefer full sun. Flower stems may be removed as they finish. Cut the whole plant to ground level as the foliage dies down in winter; if required, mulch to protect the crown of the plant from frost.

Garden-grown astilbes are usually hybrids; their colors range from raspberry-red through many shades of pink and mauve to white.

ASTRANTIA MAJOR

ASTRANTIA

Astrantias have a long flowering season throughout summer and fall, with many intricate flower heads of exquisite colors.

With their umbels of flower heads like a burst of stars, exquisite in detail and delicately colored, astrantias never fail to amaze. For this, they have long been favored by gardeners and florists alike. *Astrantia major* is the most commonly cultivated species of this small group of herbaceous perennials. The plant has a neat habit of deeply divided leaves, and grows into a clump about 2 ft (60 cm) in size, with flowering stems up to 3 ft (1 m) in height. The forms vary in flower color from white or cream tinged with green to all shades of rosy pink. In the garden, astrantias are favorably planted in drifts or at the front of mixed borders, where their captivating blooms can be frequently admired.

GROWING NOTES

Astrantia major adapts well to most garden climates, except the very hot, humid, or dry, and is tolerant of frost. The plants like full sun to slight shade, well-drained soil, and regular watering in spring and summer. The flower stems are long-lasting when cut. Divide clumps to propagate.

Among the most coveted of begonias are the tuberous hybrids (above). *Begonia fuchsioides* (right) is one of the easiest species to grow.

BEGONIA SPECIES & CULTIVARS
BEGONIA

The begonia is a tropical wonder of the exotic world. From the thousand or so species that occur throughout the tropics, especially in South America, thousands more hybrids and cultivars have evolved (most with human intervention, of course). Even the begonia's subgroups are extensive—including tuberous, shrub-like, semperflorens, and rex (which are grown exclusively for their ornate leaves).

Possibly the most coveted of begonias, but not the easiest to cultivate, are the tuberous hybrids. From species originating in the Andes (hence their need for cool, moist climates), there are now hundreds of plants in the *Begonia* x *tuberhybrida* group, each created with the aim of flowers in unspeakably beautiful colors and forms. Until recently, the best of these have been limited to specialist growers, but top-shelf types are becoming increasingly available, and adaptable.

More common in gardens are the bedding begonias, officially known as semperflorens after the species from which most of them derive. These have waxy shiny leaves and fibrous roots;

they are tough little perennials but can also be grown annually from seed. One of their ancestors, *B. fuchsioides*, with pendent red, pink, and white flowers, is a shrub-like species which is adaptable and easily grown.

The colorful semperflorens begonias have a diverse ancestry and flower range; these are among the most adaptable begonias for gardens.

GROWING NOTES

Despite their exotic nature, begonias are easy to cultivate if given suitable conditions for their group. Fancy begonias, such as tuberous or rex, may require specialized environments, but these can be replicated in greenhouses or indoors. The bedding types, however, adapt to garden climates from tropical to cool. Depending on conditions and subgroup, begonias may prefer full sun or shade. They all enjoy a moist rich soil, and can be grown in pots, too. Most begonias are easily raised from seed or propagated from cuttings.

BERGENIA SPECIES & HYBRIDS

BERGENIA

Bergenias have endeared themselves to gardeners with many valuable traits. They thrive in shade and they bloom in winter, with long-lasting clusters of flared flowers in white, purple, red, mauve, or pink. Mostly evergreen, their voluptuous foliage grows in crowded clumps of rich shapes and subtle sheens, ideal for bold edgings and ground cover. The leaves may be rounded, oval, or heart shaped; some have hairy textures or crinkled edges, while others take on cool-weather tones of deep red or burgundy. Commonly grown forms include the Siberian species *Bergenia cordifolia*, with heart-shaped leaves; the purple-flowered *B. purpurascens*; and the hybrid *B.* x *schmidtii*, which has pinky-mauve blooms.

Bergenias bring lush leaf shapes and midwinter flowers to the shady garden. *Bergenia cordifolia* (right) is one of the most popular species.

GROWING NOTES

Bergenias grow in most climates, though some are herbaceous in cold areas. The plants prefer shade or semi-shade (hot sun scorches the leaves) and well-drained rich soil. Clumps grow quickly (and may be divided) but are susceptible to snails.

Cut-leaf daisies flower in spring and summer, but they can also bloom spontaneously throughout the year.

BRACHYCOME SPECIES & HYBRIDS
CUT-LEAF DAISY

With their fine feathery leaves in low tumbling drifts that are covered in flowers for many months of the year, these little daisies from Australia have found favor in gardens all over the world. The ground-covering habit of the cut-leaf daisy is ideal for trickling over walls or rockeries, but also along paths, around garden beds, and between shrubs such as roses. These evergreen perennials are perfect for containers, too: as starring features of window boxes or hanging baskets, or as companions to standards and trees. The commonly grown species, *Brachycome multifida* and *B. iberidifolia*, include many cultivars, extending their color range from white, lilac and blue to include shades of pink, mauve, and yellow.

GROWING NOTES
Most of the cut-leaf daisies will suit climates from cool to subtropical, and also tolerate light frost. They grow and flower best in full sun, and require well-drained soil. Once established, the plants will withstand dry conditions. After flowering, trim or shear to keep the plants compact and encourage new blooms. Propagate by cuttings in the fall.

Paper daisies flower from spring to summer in the garden. For indoor arrangements, cut the flowering stems before the blooms fully open.

BRACTEANTHA BRACTEATA
PAPER DAISY

The paper daisy used to belong to the *Helichrysum* group of "everlastings," but, after many years of cultivation worldwide as a cut (and dried) flower, this Australian wildflower has struck out on its own. *Bracteantha bracteata* is a perennial, though many of the older cultivars are grown as annuals in cold climates, including 'Bright Bikini' and the Monstrosum Series, which have flower colors in red, yellow, pink, orange, and white. Recently, however, cultivators have concentrated on forms that not only feature exquisitely colored blooms, but also live longer in the garden. These include the reliable, yellow-flowered 'Dargan Hill Monarch' and 'Cockatoo,' with delicate lemon-yellow blooms.

GROWING NOTES
Paper daisies grow in all climates from cool to tropical, but prefer conditions with low humidity. The plants need full sun and very well drained soil: sandy soils enriched with organic matter are ideal. Remove the finished flowers, and lightly tip-prune young plants to keep the perennial forms compact. Plants may be propagated from seed, or from cuttings during the growing season.

CHAMELAUCIUM UNCINATUM
GERALDTON WAXFLOWER

Named after the town of Geraldton, these Western Australian wildflowers are cultivated commercially in suitable climates all over the world (from Israel to Italy to California) for their value in the cut-flower trade: the blossomy branches are extremely long-lasting. In recent years, however, their worth as garden ornamentals and potted plants has also been realised and many specialist nurseries have concentrated on performance as well as quality of bloom—improving the growing habits of new cultivars and enhancing the delicate white, cream, and pink of their flowers.

With blossomy branches throughout winter and spring, and aromatic evergreen leaves, the Geraldton waxflower is a rewarding feature in gardens and pots.

GROWING NOTES

Geraldton waxflower grows in climates from warm to cool, but thrives in low-humidity areas. The plants prefer full sun, and must have open aspects and very well drained soil (sandy or gravelly is best). Where the drainage is suspect, use raised beds or pots, as waterlogging or root rot will quickly destroy. Flowering branches may be harvested, and light pruning will keep plants compact, but avoid cutting the older wood.

DIANTHUS SPECIES & CULTIVARS
CARNATIONS & PINKS

S ome of the most successful flowering plants in the history of cultivation belong to the genus *Dianthus*, including the carnation and the pink. These perennials have, in fact, become so popular that they have each formed dynasties of their own.

The carnation has sparked craze after craze, ever since the clove-scented flower of *Dianthus caryophyllus* was used to flavor wine (a trend reportedly led, though not invented, by the first Roman emperor, Caesar Augustus). Much later, carnations became the subject of manic hybridization throughout Europe, both for the garden and as cut flowers. And while some were trade-only types never intended for gardeners, the entire flower range is now also found in the garden forms: pink, red, mauve, yellow, and white, as well as those with fringed or streaked petals.

In the everyday garden, however, of all *Dianthus*, the pinks have reigned supreme. Effortless to grow and free flowering, the cottage pinks derive from *D. plumarius*. These are also easy

In the garden, carnations mostly flower in spring and fall; pinks will flower in summer too.

Dianthus epitomize the cottage garden, where many of their best forms were developed; these fragrant flowers are also long-lasting in the vase.

to manipulate and many of their best forms were created by gardeners, including doubles, bicolors, and some with contrasting eyes or fringed petals. Most are strongly, sweetly scented and they make good cut flowers too. Another species, *D. deltoides*, the maiden pink, is also very popular, and with a mat-forming habit is often used as edging or ground cover.

GROWING NOTES

Carnations and pinks grow in warm to cool climates, and prefer low humidity especially in summer. They need full sun, protection from strong wind, and very well drained soil that is fairly alkaline and enriched with aged organic matter (added before planting). Do not overwater, and avoid overhead watering as this encourages disease. Some types are best replaced every few years, but *Dianthus* are easily propagated (and collected) from cuttings in late summer and fall.

DIASCIA SPECIES

TWINSPUR

Named for the pair of pollen sacs at the back of each flower, the twinspurs are a small group of mostly perennials from the Western Cape of South Africa, and although they haven't been long in cultivation, they are already popular in borders, rockeries, and containers. One of the most desirable species, *Diascia cordata*, is a prostrate perennial about 9 in (20 cm) in height and width: outstandingly, it flowers from late spring to early fall with dainty spires of pink blooms. Also garden-friendly is *D. rigescens*, which has a trailing habit ideal for ground cover, and mild pink blooms closely packed on upright stems throughout summer.

GROWING NOTES

Twinspurs grow in most cool to warm climates, except the tropics. They tolerate light frost but dislike humidity. In cooler areas plants prefer full sun, but in warmer gardens they require part shade, with protection from hot sun. Soil should be well drained, enriched, and moist. Water plants regularly throughout summer. Remove flower stems as they finish. Most twinspurs may be propagated from seed or cuttings.

In most twinspurs, the flowers are mild shades of pink. Some have a very long flowering season from late spring to early fall.

DIGITALIS PURPUREA & CULTIVARS
FOXGLOVE

The towering racemes of foxgloves start to unfurl their tubular flowers in spring.

What secrets hide within the foxglove's hooded spires? This woodland wildflower from Europe, the Mediterranean region, and central Asia has long charmed us with its delicate bells so daintily spotted. But the foxglove's come-hither flowers belie its deadly truth—all parts of all plants in the *Digitalis* genus are poisonous if consumed.

While in the hands of medical science, *Digitalis* plants have found some beneficial uses, especially in the treatment of heart conditions, in the hands of gardeners they have become one of the world's best-known and most-loved flowers. The foxglove typifies the cottage garden and is a favorite of the colorist's border; it is indispensable in architectural landscapes and, of course, in meadows and woodland settings.

The most recognizable of the foxgloves is *Digitalis purpurea*, with its towering racemes of purple-on-white flowers. From this species the commonly grown garden cultivars and hybrids are derived. These include series such as Foxy and Excelsior,

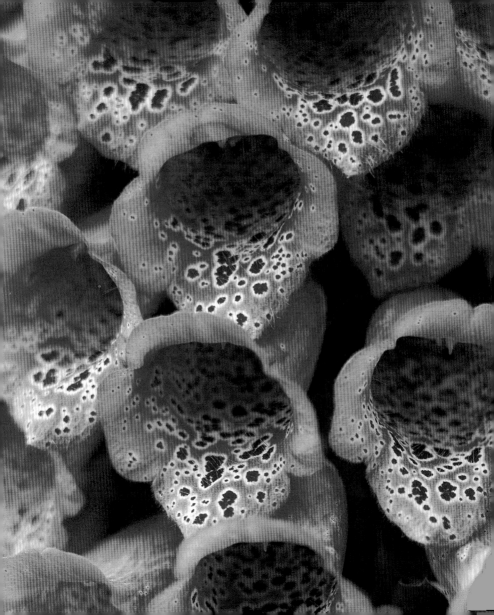

cultivars that bear the full range of modern flower colors from wine-red or apricot to ivory-white.

GROWING NOTES

Digitalis purpurea and its progeny are short-lived perennials but are often cultivated as biennials because the plants are less prolific as they age. Foxgloves will grow in most climates from cool to warm, except the tropics. The plants prefer rich, moist soil in sheltered positions, protected from hot sun or strong winds. Cutting flower stems as close to the ground as possible can induce plants to flower again later in the season. Perennial foxgloves can be grown easily by division of clumps; cultivars must be keep apart to produce reliable seed.

Cultivars and hybrids of *Digitalis purpurea* include the most delicate of pastel colors; these are tall-growing foxgloves with strong stems of flowers.

LAMIUM SPECIES
DEAD-NETTLE

W ith appealing leaves splashed with white, cream, or silver and modest but colorful flowers of mauve, yellow, or pink, dead-nettles are highly ornamental and vigorous ground covers, despite their woeful common name. Many species of *Lamium* grown in gardens also thrive in shade, where the variegated forms are especially valued for their light-reflecting leaves. Among the most popular of dead-nettles are the cultivars of *Lamium maculatum*, having both silver-marked leaves and flowers in white, mauve, or pink; and the variegated cultivar of *L. galeobdolon*, with lemon-yellow flowers, although this species can be invasive in warm gardens.

GROWING NOTES
Dead-nettles thrive in cool to warm climates, but they are less vigorous in cold gardens and not suitable for tropical areas. The plants are best in shade or part shade and well-drained soil, but will adapt to a range of conditions. Most types can spread to 6 ft (2 m), and are easily propagated by division. They can also be grown in pots, and are especially suitable for shady window boxes and hanging baskets.

Trailing perennials that enliven shady gardens, many cultivars of *Lamium* have variegated leaves as well as colorful spikes of summer flowers.

LEWISIA SPECIES
LEWISIA

Named after the American explorer Meriwether Lewis, this small group of alpine perennials was once only grown by specialists with stringently suitable conditions—those identical to the plant's native habitats of mountainous North America. Selective cultivation, however, has since produced less demanding plants, mostly derived from the evergreen species *Lewisia columbiana* and *L. cotyledon*, that are relatively trouble-free in gardens as long as their basic requirements are met—they need cool or cold climates and a fast-draining, coarse growing medium. The range of flower colors available includes red and pink to pale yellow and white, as well as those with striped flowers.

Lewisias flower in spring and early summer. Cool rockeries and alpine-style gardens provide the ideal conditions for these plants.

GROWING NOTES
Lewisias are ideally planted in rockery gardens, pockets in stone walls, or containers; mulch with gravel or crushed rock. These settings reflect their alpine origins and best display the petite rosettes of succulent leaves and delicate sprays of flower. In very cold areas, the plants require full sun; in cool climates, they prefer part shade. Do not overwater at any time, and keep plants as dry as possible in winter.

LUPINUS POLYPHYLLUS & HYBRIDS
RUSSELL LUPINS

Before the English gardener George Russell started fiddling with lupins, on his allotment in York around 1910, varieties of *Lupinus polyphyllus* were already in circulation. A herbaceous wildflower of North America, this perennial lupin was a success almost from the moment it landed on European shores (a century or so before Russell's time) and cultivars soon appeared. These were, however, rather limited to a color range of purple, blue, and occasionally white.

George Russell gathered together many lupins on his allotment—including cultivars of *Lupinus polyphyllus* and the Mexican species *L. hartwegii*—and left them to their own pollination devices. For more than 20 years Russell stringently selected the seedlings, then he exhibited some of his cultivars—flowers in pure red, pink, orange, and yellow, and bicolors of blue-and-yellow and purple-and-pink—and the ornamental lupin was never the same again.

Since they first appeared in 1937, Russell hybrids have set a high standard for all ornamental lupins.

Russell lupins flower from late spring to early summer. Removing the finished flower stems encourages a second flush of blooms.

Since the Russell hybrids debuted in 1937, they have defined the ornamental lupin. Apart from their range of color, the plants are vigorous, with large palmate leaves that form attractive clumps. They can also produce many flowering stems, each strong and straight, up to 3 ft (1 m) in height, and densely packed with blooms.

GROWING NOTES

Russell lupins prefer cool climates. In warmer regions, they are less floriferous and often treated as annuals. The plants grow in full sun or part shade, and require well-drained soil and protection from wind. They are intolerant of humidity or waterlogging. Even in ideal conditions, Russell lupins may be short-lived, but are easily propagated from cuttings or seed. Like all members of the legume family, lupins have beneficial effects on the nitrogen levels of the soil in which they are grown.

LYTHRUM CULTIVARS
LOOSESTRIFE

Naturally lovely as the wild forms of loosestrife may be, with their slender spires of purple or red flowers, the *Lythrum* species have long been surpassed in gardens by their cultivars. The purple loosestrife, *Lythrum salicaria*, may be widely distributed around waterways of Europe and temperate Asia, but most gardeners prefer its many named varieties—especially the flowers of subdued pink which are easily placed among other plants. Another species, *L. virgatum*, is also less favored than its cultivars: 'Rose Queen,' with deep pink flowers, is one of the most popular of these. All these commonly grown *Lythrum* are herbaceous perennials that form clumps of lance-shaped leaves and produce their towering spires in summer.

The subdued pink spires of loosestrife cultivars are especially effective when placed in meadowy drifts or near water.

GROWING NOTES

Loosestrife grows in most cool to temperate climates, in full sun to part shade, but must have rich, moist soil. Marginal conditions, damp borders, and marshy meadows are ideal, and the plants look especially good near water (as in their natural habitats). The species will set seed freely, but cultivars are best propagated by division.

MALVA SPECIES
MALLOW

Even though its name is given to a large family (Malvaceae) which includes the hibiscus, lantern flower, cotton plant, and hollyhock, the true mallows from the genus *Malva* are limited in the garden to a few species of annuals, biennials, and perennials. These are distinguished by their five-petaled flowers, saucer shaped or funnel-like and fluted, in a range of soft pink hues. The musk mallow, *Malva moschata*, is a tall, branching perennial of Europe and northern Africa, aptly named for the musk scent of the plant (which intensifies in warm weather), but also for its flower color (though this may vary from white to dark pink). Another perennial, *M. alcea*, with flowers of cool pinks ranging towards mauve, is also ornamental and sometimes known as the hollyhock mallow.

The musk pink to mauve flowers of the perennial mallows will open in succession, for months from early summer.

GROWING NOTES
The perennial types of mallow suit most climates except the tropics. They prefer full sun, though in warmer regions will grow in part shade. The plants tend to form upright branching clumps, up to 3 ft (1 m) tall. They can be short-lived but are easily divided for propagation.

OENOTHERA SPECIES & CULTIVARS
EVENING PRIMROSE

Most perennial evening primroses, such as the pink-flowered form of *Oenothera speciosa*, flower from late spring to summer and are gently fragrant.

Though it has immense therapeutic powers, the herbally known evening primrose (*Oenothera biennis*), a wildflower of northern America, is a fairly scruffy-looking yellow-flowered biennial with weedy tendencies, and is not often seen in domestic gardens. Its perennial relations, however, are highly valued for ornamental purposes, with their delicate cupped blooms in gentle colors and more affable growing habits. These include white evening primrose, *O. speciosa*, though its pink-flowered forms are possibly more popular than the species; the trailing *O. acaulis*, with white flowers that turn pink as they age; and *O. tetragona*, which has yellow flowers on red stems, some with scarlet stamens to match.

GROWING NOTES

Most perennial evening primroses are easy to grow in many climates from warm to cool. They prefer full sun all day (but will make do with half a day), and well-drained soil. Regular watering promotes growth and a good flowering display. Some of the perennials, such as *O. speciosa*, can be short-lived, but easily renew from rhizomes or seeds.

OSTEOSPERMUM SPECIES & CULTIVARS
VELDT DAISY

The veldt daisy from South Africa has distinctively colored flower heads that make it one of the most desirable of the 'African daisies' (a name given to many). *Osteospermum* is also very adaptable to cultivation, growing in evergreen mounds 1–2 ft (30–60 cm) in size, and suitable for ground cover, sweeping drifts, pots, and streetscapes. The best-loved veldt daisies include *Osteospermum ecklonis*, which has flower heads with blue centers and white ray florets streaked blue on the undersides; and *O. barberae*, with blooms that are cerise and blue. In the cultivars, the quilled 'Whirligig' is really cute; while 'Buttermilk' has blooms of creamy-yellow contrasted with chocolate-brown centers.

GROWING NOTES

Veldt daisies grow in all climates from tropical to cool, but need protection from heavy frost. The plants prefer full sun all day and well-drained soil; they also tolerate exposed windy sites and infrequent watering once established. They are easily propagated from cuttings; in cold climates, for overwintering, establish these before the fall. Clip or shear plants after flowering to keep them compact, and prune as required. The flowers aren't suitable for cutting, only opening in full sun.

Veldt daisies flower profusely from late winter throughout spring and summer, depending on the garden's climate.

PAEONIA SPECIES & CULTIVARS
PEONY

Cultivated for thousands of years, the peony flower remains a gardener's prize.

The peony is more than a flower, it is a flowering prize—it was first cultivated in China, where the ancestral *Paeonia lactiflora* originates; then in Japan, where the coveted blooms arrived around the eighth century; and finally it was introduced to Europe, in the 1800s, and the rest of the world.

From only about 30 species of *Paeonia*, there are many hundreds of cultivars and these are broadly classified as tree or herbaceous. The tree peonies derive from *P. suffruticosa*, the moutan (from the Chinese for "most beautiful"), and are shrub-like and grow to about 6 ft (2 m) tall. The herbaceous peonies, mostly descendants of *P. lactiflora*, are more compact, only growing to 3 ft (1 m) or so in width and height. Peony cultivars are then divided into official categories based on flower type, including single, double, and anemone-flowered.

Peonies represent every luscious hue of red, purple, pink, cream, and white known to flowers. Some have prominent stamens; others show contrasts, or are deeply saturated and pure in hue. The petal forms can vary, and may be fluted, picoteed, or frilled. Of course, many peonies are also fragrant.

The leafy habit of peonies, often overshadowed by the blooms, looks lush in the garden, too. Depending on the cultivar, peonies can flower in spring or summer.

GROWING NOTES

Peonies prefer cool to cold climates, though some will flower in warmer areas as long as their basic dormancy needs (two months at least) are met. The plants require full sun to semi-shade, protection from strong wind, and well-drained soil that is rich and friable. Water generously throughout spring and summer. Remove flowers as they finish, but only trim back foliage after it has naturally died down. Plants strengthen and become more prolific as they age, so while clumps may be divided for propagation, they are best left for 5–10 years.

PHLOX SPECIES & CULTIVARS

PHLOX

Phlox paniculata is a tall-growing perennial species with many colored forms and fragrant flowers.

Phlox is one of the star attractions of the summer flower garden, with flashy-colored flower heads produced in profusion and creating a tremendous impact throughout the season. The commonly grown perennial phlox, *Phlox paniculata*, forms a tall clump and has rounded inflorescences of fragant flowers in an enormous range of colors, including red, orange, pink, mauve, purple, and white, some with contrasting eyes. Lesser known but no less appealing are the prostrate perennials, which are low-growing phloxes with a ground-covering habits. The most popular of these is *P. subulata*, an evergreen sometimes called alpine or moss phlox, with flower colors that may be white, pink, lilac, or mauve.

GROWING NOTES

Phlox paniculata thrives in a wide range of climates, from warm to cool, and has an easy-growing herbaceous habit that is ideal for borders as well as pots. As its name suggests, the alpine phlox prefers cool to cold climates. Both types are best in full sun. Propagate by division of plants or root cuttings.

Perennial forms of primrose include the candelabra types, with tiers of blooms.

PRIMULA SPECIES & CULTIVARS
PRIMROSE

The primrose family (Primulaceae) is extensive and includes about 400 species which span the temperate parts of the northern hemisphere. Apart from the natural forms, there are also many hundreds of hybrids and cultivars. As a result of all this complexity and the sheer numbers, subgroups of *Primula* have formed. These include the candelabras (primroses with tiers of flowers in whorls up the stem), the polyanthus (the modern hybrid of potted color fame), and the auriculas (the fancy primroses of shows and societies, long distinguished as a class of their own).

In the garden, there are many perennial species, varieties, and hybrids that are also highly valued for their ease of cultivation. These vary greatly and include the European wildflowers *Primula vulgaris*, the common primrose, and *P. veris*, the cowslip (these two combine in polyanthus); the drumstick primula, *P. denticulata*, with its pompom-style

Primula vulgaris (left), the European wildflower, is the ancestor of many modern primroses, including polyanthus. *P. obconica* (opposite) has flowers in a range of pastel tones.

clusters; the pastel-flowered cultivars of the Chinese *P. obconica* (these aren't allergenic like the species); and the cherry-blossom primrose, *P. sieboldii*, from Japan, which has some forms with picotee-edged petals.

GROWING NOTES

Perennial primroses are generally adaptable and thrive in cool to warm climates in moist, rich soils. Most grow in sun or part shade, as well as pots. Some of the border types, like *P. vulgaris* and *P. obconica*, tend to last only a few years (naturally seeding or spreading from basal clumps). Others, like the fairy primrose (*P. malacoides*) and polyanthus (*P.* x *polyantha*), can be so short-lived that they are grown as annuals or potted color, especially in warmer climates. Removing the finished blooms of primroses helps to extend their flowering. Clumps of perennial types may be divided for propagation; self-sown seedlings can be prolific and provide colorful surprises.

REHMANNIA ELATA
CHINESE FOXGLOVE

The Chinese foxglove belongs to a very small genus of herbaceous perennials from eastern Asia, and while it looks very much like a foxglove (and was once classified as part of that family), the plants are actually related to African violets (*Saintpaulia*). Only one species of *Rehmannia* is commonly cultivated in gardens: *R. elata* has large, divided, hairy leaves forming a generous basal clump, and in flower the plants can grow to 3–5 ft (1–1.5 m) in height. The blooms are bright pink in the species, but vary to mauve, and unfurl gradually along the flowering stem, providing long-lasting spires of summer and fall color.

The flowers of the Chinese foxglove, *Rehmannia elata*, gradually open on tall and slender spires.

GROWING NOTES

Chinese foxgloves grow best in warm-temperate to cool climates. In cooler areas, they prefer full sun; in warmer gardens, they need part shade (especially in summer). The plants require rich, well-drained soil, and shelter from strong wind. Water regularly to establish, and during the growing season. *Rehmannia elata* tends to be short-lived even in ideal conditions, but is easily propagated from seed or root cuttings.

RHODOHYPOXIS BAURII

ROSE GRASS

In a symphony of pinks, the flowers of rose grass appear in spring; with some cultivars, the colors change as the flowers age.

When rose grass flowers, it puts on a symphony of starry pink that has gardeners in raptures. The flowers are unique (with a three-on-three petal formation), and produced in such numbers that they completely obscure the plant's foliage. It's a performance that lasts for weeks, from spring until late summer; and in sweet colors, too—from deep to pale pink and also sugary white, sometimes with tiny highlights of cerise. Endemic to the south-eastern corner of South Africa, and found at high altitudes, this tuberous perennial has grass-like leaves and grows to about 4 in (10 cm) tall. It has a natural affinity with stone gardens and rockeries, but can also be planted at the front of borders, and in pots.

GROWING NOTES

Rose grass will grow in warm to cool climates, and prefers full sun. The soil should be very well drained, rich with aged organic matter, and acidic. The plants need plenty of water in summer while growing, less in the fall as the foliage dies off, and a dry winter dormancy. Propagate by dividing clumps.

SILENE SPECIES & CULTIVARS
SILENE

Extensively distributed throughout the fields and woodlands of Europe and Africa, *Silene* is a large genus of annuals, biennials, and perennials, commonly known as sea campion or catchfly. All silenes have simple five-petaled flowers, mostly in tones of purple and red to pink and white. While many species are rare in cultivation, and a few are cast as weeds, there are also several garden-worthy perennials such as *Silene dioica*, and its double-flowered cultivar 'Rosea Plena,' and *S. schafta*, which grows in low drifts. Their simple panicles of flower add a soft, informal touch to rockeries and edging, as well as cottage gardens and mixed borders.

GROWING NOTES
The commonly grown silenes suit a variety of climates, but in general they dislike tropical or humid environments and prefer warm dry summers and cool to cold winters. Most of the perennials are herbaceous and frost hardy. They require full sun or slightly shaded conditions, and a light sandy soil. Propagate by dividing clumps.

Most perennial silenes flower from spring throughout summer; the blooms may be followed by bauble-like fruits.

SISYRINCHIUM SPECIES
SATIN GRASS

Though many of the *Sisyrinchium* species are commonly called grasses, this small genus originating in North and South America actually belongs to the iris family (Iridaceae). Like many irises, they have long sword-shaped leaves growing in fanned clumps, but *Sisyrinchium* are more demure. The smallest species, *S. bellum*, forms a tiny tuft only about 4 in (10 cm) in height (ideal for rockeries); with violet-blue flowers, it looks like a miniature iris. One of the largest types, *S. striatum*, grows to 2 ft (60 cm) tall, and, unlike most irises, bears its many blooms along its tall, elegant spike. The flowers, appearing in summer, are pale yellow with purple stripes on the reverse side of the petals, and there is also a variegated form with cream-striped leaves.

The summer blooms of *Sisyrinchium striatum*, sometimes known as the satin flower, emerge on tall spires from clumps of sword-like leaves.

GROWING NOTES

Most perennial types of *Sisyrinchium* grow in cool to warm climates, but prefer cooler areas. Many are also tolerant of frost. The plants like full sun (though some take part shade), and well-drained soil. Species may self-seed, but all types can be propagated by dividing clumps.

THALICTRUM SPECIES
MEADOW RUE

The pink fluffy display for which meadow rue is best known is performed without a single petal. Instead, the flowers of *Thalictrum* are formed by prominent sepals and stamens that conspire to appear fringed; mostly pink in the species, and white or mauve in cultivars. Although the flowering tends to be short, in spring or early summer, the leaves of meadow rue are decorative for many months—being lofty, fern-like, and lobed—and grow quickly into clumps about 3 ft (1 m) in size. *Thalictrum aquilegiifolium*, with flamboyantly fringed blooms, is the most commonly grown of the perennials; however, *T. delavayi* is also popular for its super-fine foliage and loose panicles of nodding starry flowers.

GROWING NOTES

These perennial types will grow in most climates, except the tropics. They prefer light shade, or morning sun only, in warmer gardens, but like full sun in cool climates. The soil should be well drained but organically enriched. Water generously throughout spring and summer. Remove flower stems as they finish, and cut the plant to just above ground level as foliage dies down in the fall.

The delicate flowers and leaves of meadow rue are especially effective in lightly shaded gardens. *Thalictrum delavayi* (right) has starry flowers and super-fine leaves.

VERBASCUM SPECIES & CULTIVARS
VERBASCUM

Many of the garden-grown hybrids derive from *Verbascum phoeniceum,* and flower in spring and summer.

Surely there are few flowers as naturally elegant as the verbascum, with its lofty spires of bloom. Unlike many of their relations (including foxgloves), the verbascum's flowers are simply five-lobed, and look like blossoms. In some types of verbascum, the flower stems are branched, with the branches simultaneously bearing blooms, while in others the spike is singular. The flowers open a few at a time, in tight bunches, and always sit close to the stems, giving verbascum its distinctively slender style.

Although a few species of these evergreen perennials have naturalized in various parts of the world, in particular *Verbascum thapsus* (the mullein of Europe, Asia, and America), most of the commonly grown garden types never escape their ornamental realms. The species *V. phoeniceum* and its hybrids are immensely popular, growing to about 5 ft (1.5 m) tall in flower, with a range of appealing colors that includes lilac, red, white, yellows (from lemon to golden), and soft shades of orange and pink. With singular spikes of purple-centered yellow flowers from late summer through fall, *V. nigrum* is also well known. And uniquely spectacular is the tall and

Verbascums always make an impact, but these perennials are also easy to grow and adaptable. *Verbascum olympicum* (opposite) is one of the more spectacular species.

yellow-flowering *V. olympicum*, with large, pale gray-green leaves forming a rosette from which the candelabra-like flower stem emerges—clothed in silvery-white hairs, the plant has a spectral glow.

GROWING NOTES

Evergreen or herbaceous, most perennial verbascums can be grown in cool to warm climates, but prefer conditions that are dry with low rainfall. They require full sun all day (the spires will be disappointing otherwise) and adapt to any well-drained soil. Water regularly to establish the plants, after which they are resistant to periods of drought. Some types of verbascum are short-lived and treated as biennials. Cultivars should be propagated from root cuttings.

neutral

Neutral colors aren't really colors but more like moments of light. The neutrals are the chameleons of the garden—the colors you have when you don't have color. Neutrals include the infinite shades of white, from waxy and creamy to metallic or diaphanous, all the verdant tones of green, and also silvers, metallic colours and grays.

Though often based on green and white, neutral-toned gardens can also use other colors to enhance designs. PREVIOUS PAGES: A white variation of the purple coneflower, *Echinacea purpurea* 'Alba.'

Neutral-colored gardens are increasingly desirable: notably the "white," "silver," and "green" gardens. However, these color schemes are also popular because they are easy to design and easy on the eye. They are adaptable, enduring, enlightened, and create a sense of spaciousness. Neutral colors in gardens are transient, too, depending on the surroundings and the seasons.

Neutral colors are elegant and enlightening, but they are also easy to include in garden designs. RIGHT: A white form of the Madagascar periwinkle, *Catharanthus roseus*.

This chapter features flowering perennials in neutral colors. But note that many flowers in this book will have a white form. And, don't forget the importance of foliage in these schemes—whether green, silver, or gray, leaves set the theme. Nor should you overlook the use of other colors, as a deliberate splash of something bold or bright will often enhance a neutral-toned design.

Neutral-colored flowers bring light and space to the garden. FOLLOWING PAGES: White is the first flower color to appear at dawn and the last to fade at night. It is also the brightest in shade.

ACANTHUS MOLLIS
ACANTHUS

The acanthus is a plant not known for color but for form. Just ask any artist—from the creators of the Greek Corinthian columns topped with acanthus foliage reliefs, or the Arts and Crafts designers who carved, wove and painted its image, to the gardeners of the past and present, who honor the plant in their garden designs. And it's not just a matter of size, though in the garden *Acanthus mollis* can grow into a beefy clump. Whether we admire its long-lasting and notable spires of burgundy and white flowers, or its famously shaped and shiny leaf, or the plant's overall outstanding appearance, the acanthus is an inspiring feature wherever it grows.

GROWING NOTES

Also known as bear's breeches or oyster plant, these herbaceous perennials originate in the Mediterranean region but are adaptable to climates from cool to tropical. They are best in shade or semi-shade, and well-drained soil that is moist and enriched. Water generously in spring and summer while the plants are growing and flowering. Clumps grow quickly, though they are dormant in winter, and may be divided.

Acanthus should be planted where its outstanding form makes a great impact, such as under trees, in shaded borders, against walls or stone, or in pots.

ALCHEMILLA MOLLIS
LADY'S MANTLE

Few flowering perennials are better purveyors of pure green in the garden than the lady's mantle, *Alchemilla mollis*. Although the genus name, *Alchemilla*, means "little magical one" (mostly in reference to the dew-collecting abilities of the leaves), the common species *A. mollis* is more known for garden prowess than curative qualities. A herbaceous perennial, it has funnel-shaped, wavy-edged leaves, with a silvery green velvety texture, that overlap in light clumps about 1 ft (30 cm) in height. The blooms appear in late spring or summer in billows of fluorescent yellow-green—actually an effect of colorful bracts, not flowers.

Lady's mantle flowers in long-lasting billows of luminous bright green, but the leaves are highly ornamental too.

GROWING NOTES

Alchemilla mollis is best in cool to cold climates, in full sun, but it adapts to warmer areas, in part shade, as long as high humidity is avoided. The plants require rich, well-drained soil and regular watering in spring and summer (like rain and dew, the effect of hosing is sparkling). Remove flowering stems as they finish, and cut back plants when foliage dies down. Clumps can be divided, but the plants will also self-seed, and seedlings are easily transplanted.

ANEMONE X HYBRIDA
JAPANESE WINDFLOWER

E ver since they were created, in the horticultural hotbeds of Europe around the mid-1800s, these hybrid windflowers have eclipsed their parent species, *Anemone hupehensis*, the real Japanese windflower (which is actually Chinese, but also long cultivated in Japan). Though this pink-flowered species and its selected cultivars are still popular, most of the Japanese windflowers in gardens are forms of *A. x hybrida*.

Most of the windflowers grown in gardens are Anemone x hybrida, with flower colors from cerise to blushing pink to pure white.

Herbaceous perennials, these shade-lovers are naturally suited to woodland gardens and other gently lit schemes. Their tri-lobed, maple-like leaves grow in airy clumps that spread in drifts, via underground stems (which are easily removed, if necessary). The plants have a timely flowering season, from late summer to early fall, when many other perennials are starting to fade. With their fine panicles up to 3 ft (1 m) in height, they form a lofty and long-lasting display.

The blooms, typically anemone with fluttery petals and fine stamen clusters, may be deep pink to palest blush to white, depending on the cultivar, and there are also single and double forms. 'Honorine Jobert,' with pure white petals and yellow stamens around a green cushiony center, arose as a mutation at a French nursery in the 1850s, and is still one of the most popular cultivars today.

GROWING NOTES

Japanese windflowers are easy to grow in climates from warm to cool. They prefer moist conditions, and shade or part shade, with shelter from strong winds. The soil should be well drained and enriched for good growth. Remove flower stems as they finish and cut back the plant to ground level as the foliage dies down. Clumps may be divided for propagation, but make sure that each section has strong roots.

Japanese windflowers have a long flowering season, from late summer to fall. The plants are naturally suited to shady borders and woodland-style gardens.

ARABIS CAUCASICA
ROCK CRESS

The rock cress is related to stock, as can be seen (and sometimes smelt) in the flowers, but it also belongs to the same family (Brassicaceae) as broccoli, cabbage, and kale. Of the many *Arabis* species, mostly from Europe and Asia, only one frequents the garden: the white-flowering *Arabis caucasica* (syn. *A. albida*), and its double-flowered or pink cultivars. This mat-forming perennial, growing to about 6 in (15 cm) in height, is often featured in rockeries, stone gardens, informal edging, and low borders, where it spreads swiftly in leafy rosettes. The plants flower from midwinter until late summer, and, if set in a drift, the effect is fragrant and cloud-like.

GROWING NOTES

Rock cress is best in cool to cold climates, but also grows in warm areas as long as humidity is low. The plants must have full sun and very well drained soil. Once established, they tolerate infrequent watering but do require a drink if spring and summer are very dry. Cut back plants after flowering to keep them compact, and propagate clumps by division.

Rock cress blooms from midwinter to summer. Cultivars include those with double-petalled or pink flowers.

ARENARIA SPECIES
SANDWORT

Glistening white flowers on small rounded cushions of gray-green leaves make *Arenaria* one of the most charming of rockery-style perennials. Often found in sandy mountainous habitats, in the Mediterranean region and western Europe, most *Arenaria* species are naturally suited to intimately scaled stone gardens, rockeries, and raised beds, and also containers such as bowls and troughs. Some of the alpines form hard mounds that are less than 2 in (5 cm) tall. The largest species, *Arenaria montana*, spreads to about 2 ft (60 cm) in width, but only grows 4 in (10 cm) in height. This adaptable perennial is the most commonly seen in gardens, and, apart from their rock-related uses, the soft tumbling drifts of *A. montana* are also ideal for edging, pots, and low borders.

Arenaria montana forms a soft drift of gray-green leaves with glistening white spring flowers; it is ideal for mixed edging and low borders, as well as in rockeries and pots.

GROWING NOTES

All species of *Arenaria* prefer full sun in cool to cold climates, and are very tolerant of frost. Some, like *A. montana*, will also adapt to more temperate areas or suitable microclimates in warm gardens, but they will need some shade. The plants must have very well drained, sandy soil. Divide clumps or take cuttings for propagation.

CATHARANTHUS ROSEUS
MADAGASCAR PERIWINKLE

Once thrown in with other periwinkles (and formerly classified as *Vinca rosea*), the Madagascar periwinkle, though poisonous if consumed, has been found to contain certain cancer-fighting agents and is now cultivated commercially for its alkaloids, as well as in gardens for its ornamental value. Long proven as easy-growing in mixed borders, stand-alone masses or pots, the plant has an upright habit, about 1 ft (30 cm) tall, and near-succulent, dark green leaves that well display its mass of flowers. These have five petals, mostly in soft pink to red or white, with darker-toned eyes. The white-flowered form is made even more outstanding by its crimson center, which sharpens the pristine petal color.

Madagascar periwinkles flower in late spring or summer; the flowers are mostly shades of pink to red but also include an outstanding white with crimson center.

GROWING NOTES

Madagascar periwinkles are evergreen in tropical and warm conditions but sometimes grown as annuals, especially in cool climates. The plants grow in full sun or semi-shade, though the paler-colored flowers are better when shaded. The soil should be well drained but quite rich and moist; avoid any waterlogging. Replace plants as they become less prolific. They are easily propagated from cuttings or seed.

CERASTIUM TOMENTOSUM
SNOW-IN-SUMMER

This ground covering perennial flowers from spring to summer, creating a low drift of white and silvery green.

Snow-in-summer is a tiny ground cover that tumbles along in the garden and named for the way it creates a winter wonderland effect with its snowflake-white flowers and silvery shimmer of leaves. Growing only to about 4 in (10 cm) in height, this prostrate perennial has trailing stems that send down roots as they grow. The plant can spread infinitely, and in ideal conditions, such as in Mediterranean climates, it can become invasive. It is often planted in rockery pockets or on steep slopes to stabilize the soil, and its furry gray-green leaves make it an attractive ground cover all year round.

GROWING NOTES

Cerastium tomentosum revels in sunny, dry, and well-drained conditions in warm or cool climates. It sulks in shade or wet soil, and is unsuitable for tropical areas or those with high summer rainfall. To keep plants tidy, use shears to trim the finished flowers. Prune regularly to encourage plants to grow densely, and cut back hard if they start to creep out of control. Plants are easily propagated from cuttings or by division.

CONVALLARIA MAJALIS

LILY-OF-THE-VALLEY

In the same way that lily-of-the-valley upgrades a posy, or adds a magical undernote to perfumes, the plants transform shaded gardens into enchanted places. Naturally found in the northern hemisphere, with an affinity for woodlands, lilies-of-the-valley grow from small fleshy rhizomes (called pips), with large, fluidly shaped leaves, and form lush ground covers; the plants can also be grown in pots and brought indoors in flower. The flowers are highlights of spring: white bells in the species, but cultivars include pale pink or double blooms.

Apart from their value to perfumery and floristry, lilies-of-the-valley transform shady gardens into magical places with their verdant leaves and alluring flowers.

GROWING NOTES

Lilies-of-the-valley prefer cool to cold climates. In warmer gardens they can disappoint with limpid leaves and few flowers. Plants prefer full shade to filtered (ideal for naturalizing under trees), and the soil should be well drained but rich in aged organic matter. Clumps may be divided for propagation, but are better left undisturbed for several years. For arrangements, cut the sprays when nearly all flowers are opened.

CRASSULA SPECIES
JADE PLANT

The jade plants thrive where many others wouldn't dare to grow, but these succulent perennials, mostly from South Africa but also Madagascar and South America, are highly ornamental, too—many with unusual leaves as well as clusters of star-shaped flowers. Much favored is the silver jade plant, *Crassula arborescens*, which has gray-green rounded leaves, sometimes with red margins, and pale pink flowers: it can eventually reach a spectacular 9 ft (3 m) tall. Also popular, *C. multicava* grows more like ground cover, and even in minimal soil its spreading stems can establish roots; in spring, these leathery-leaved clumps bear branched stems of long-lasting flowers which are pink in bud but open starry white.

The tall-growing *Crassula arborescens* (above), like many jade plants, thrives in pots. *C. multicava* (right) has a ground-covering habit, and flourishes in rocky crevices.

GROWING NOTES

Most jade plants are extremely adaptable to climates from near-tropical to cool, but are best in warm or temperate frost-free gardens (many also grow in pots, indoors or outside). They generally prefer full sun but tolerate some shading, and require well-drained soil. Depending on the type, plants are very easily propagated from stem cuttings or by division.

CYMBIDIUM HYBRIDS
CYMBIDIUM ORCHID

The orchid family, Orchidaceae, is the second largest of flowering plants (after daisies). But in terms of hybrids and cultivars, the orchids outrank anything in cultivation. Cymbidiums, for their worldwide popularity both as cut flowers and in the garden, have won themselves the title of King of the Orchids, and in this genus alone there are thousands of cultivars.

Cymbidiums have been known since at least the time of Confucius, who particularly admired their *lan* (fragrance). They are now so popular that cymbidiums have their own societies and shows (apart from orchid-related ones); and the cultivars are so numerous that they are divided into three broad categories—miniature, intermediate, and standard (although based on flower dimensions, often these also indicate the plant's overall size). Among them are flowers in

Cymbidium flower spikes, produced from early fall to late spring, depending on the cultivar, can last for months; if potted, the whole plant may be brought indoors.

every conceivable shade of red, pink, white, yellow, orange, brown, and even a range of greens; some beautifully marked with contrasting lips or stripes.

A cymbidium grower's rule of thumb is that cultivars with paler-colored flowers require more shade, while those with darker blooms need more light.

GROWING NOTES

Cymbidiums are among the easiest orchids to grow and adapt well to pots, shadehouses, and temperate gardens. They have a few basic requirements including high humidity year round; cool winter temperatures, not below about 40°F (5°C); and warm (not hot) summers. A distinct difference between day and night temperatures initiates flowering. The plants also need full sun in winter but shade in summer. The soil or potting medium must be very fast draining and light (such as aged pine bark chunks), but kept moist.

Cymbidiums are true perennials, with original clumps capable of going on for decades (and passed down through generations of orchid growers). It is best to obtain plants from reputable sources who can also provide cultivation advice, such as local societies and specialist nurseries.

EREMURUS SPECIES & HYBRIDS
FOXTAIL LILY

From Asia and the Middle East, the foxtail lily is also known as desert candles or king's spear—all common names which appropriately describe the plant's outstanding flower spires. These are tapered racemes of closely packed, starry, tiny flowers, glowing white, pink, orange-red, or yellow as they gradually open. The plants generally grow in rosettes of strap-like leaves (which die down after flowering), each one producing a single spectacular flower stem that can be up to 6 ft (2 m) tall. Commonly grown in gardens are the pink-flowering species *Eremurus robustus* and *E. olgae*; the pure white *E. himalaicus*; and hybrids such as the Shelford series, which includes most of the flower colors.

GROWING NOTES
All types of *Eremurus* prefer cool to cold climates and are very resistant to frost. The plants require full sun, protection from strong wind, and well-drained soil. The clumps are best left undisturbed for many years, but may be divided for propagation (take care as the fleshy roots are fragile). Seedlings may take years to reach flowering size.

Most of the foxtail lilies flower throughout summer: each tall and tapered spire is tightly packed with tiny starry blooms.

ERIGERON SPECIES & CULTIVARS
FLEABANE

Erigeron karvinskianus can bloom throughout the year and grows into a ground covering flower carpet.

The Erigeron daisies are trailing perennials that mostly originate from North and South America, but their adaptability to cultivation has ensured their success worldwide. So much so that the most commonly seen species, *Erigeron karvinskianus*, with blooms that change from white to pink to purple as they age, has been declared noxious in some countries. There are, however, other species, hybrids, and cultivars of fleabane (a forklore-ish reference to the plants' supposed ability to repel fleas) which also provide effortless displays without becoming a menace. These include the yellow-flowered species *E. aureus*, and the cultivar *E.* 'Charity,' with blooms of pale pink ray florets and green-yellow centers.

GROWING NOTES

Erigeron daisies thrive in most climates except the tropics and dry inland areas. Most prefer full sun, but *E. karvinskianus* likes some shade. The plants require well-drained soil and protection from strong wind. They can be short-lived, but are easily propagated from seed (or by self-seeding) as well as by division. Cut back immediately after flowering to keep growth compact, and also to prevent seeds from forming.

ERYNGIUM SPECIES & CULTIVARS
SEA HOLLY

The flower heads of sea holly, apart from being striking with spiky bracts, have an unusual color range of steely blues, verdigris, pewter, silver, and mercurial white. The leaves are sharply divided, almost jagged, often spiny, and borne in basal clumps. The whole arrangement of *Eryngium* looks dangerously exciting—these are plants that define the gardens around them. Many species and cultivars are available, including those with metallic blue flower heads, such as *Eryngium maritimum* and *E. planum*; and also those of silver and white, such as *E. variifolium*, with blooms like abstract stars. Sea hollies should always be planted in full sun for best growth and because it adds to their unearthly glow.

GROWING NOTES

Most *Eryngium* in gardens are herbaceous perennials. They adapt to climates from subtropical to cool, but need full sun and very well drained soil (preferably sandy). Some of the taller types should be staked in flower, being 9–12 ft (1.5–2 m) in height. Clumps may be divided (though are prickly to handle). The flower heads are long-lasting when cut, and keep their form and color when dried.

The flowers and foliage forms of sea hollies define gardens with dramatic shapes and metallic colors.

With its unique formation of stems and leaves, *Euphorbia trigona* (above) makes a dramatic indoor plant. *E. characias* subsp. *wulfenii* (right) is a tall, evergreen perennial.

EUPHORBIA SPECIES
EUPHORBIA

One of the largest families of flowering plants, euphorbia includes many curious characters. Members of the genus are known for their caustic sap, and go by unflattering common names such as milkweed or spurge. Among them are plants with spines, horns, thorns, knobs, and nipples. There's *Euphorbia tirucalli*, with alien, green, pencil-like protrusions; *E. caput-medusae*, the Medusa's head; and *E. milii*, the crown of thorns. The most popular euphorbias, however, are grown for their unusually beautiful leaves and flower bracts, including the poinsettia, *E. pulcherrima*, the creamy-white *E. marginata*, and *E. characias* subsp. *wulfenii*, a luminous lime-green.

Apart from their wondrous forms and colors, euphorbias come highly recommended as garden plants. The perennials

with shrubby habits and whorls of evergreen leaves, such as *Euphorbia robbiae* and *E. characias* subsp. *wulfenii*, provide lucid contrasts in mixed borders or as backgrounds for other plants. Euphorbias are also striking as specimens, or in pots; settings which fully exploit their other-worldly qualities.

GROWING NOTES

Euphorbias have worldwide origins, with species from the Mediterranean and Europe to Asia, South Africa, and Mexico, and the family includes annuals, perennials, and shrub-types for almost all climates except the extremely wet or cold. Most euphorbias need sunny and well-drained aspects, but they will also tolerate the poorest of soils and long periods of drought. Those with succulent leaves are especially tough, and many of these make outstanding indoor pot plants.

Euphorbias require minimal attention once established, but will respond to regular watering and pruning back of old flower spikes. If you are attending to them, take precautions with their irritating sap. Most species grow readily from seed (a few have become localized noxious weeds), and perennial types can be easily propagated from cuttings.

The spring inflorescences of perennial euphorbias are long-lasting; in the garden, these plants can be used to create great drifts of surreal beauty.

GAURA LINDHEIMERI
GAURA

From southern North America, gauras are mostly prairie wildflowers and related to the evening primrose. Their name *Gaura* means "superb," describing these plants in flower. The perennial *Gaura lindheimeri* is the only species in cultivation, and much favored in cottage gardens, mixed borders, and meadow styles. The plant grows in large dense clumps of lance-shaped leaves and has fine, branched flowering stems, up to 4 ft (1.2 m) in height. The five-petaled blooms begin as pink buds and open white with pink calyx tubes, but an all-pink cultivar has recently been produced. Gauras can bloom from spring and summer to fall, creating a long-lasting haze of starry flowers.

Gauras are trouble-free in most climates and have a long flowering season; fine panicles in prolific numbers create a haze of white-and-pink blooms.

GROWING NOTES

Gaura lindheimeri is easy to grow in most climates from cool to warm and subtropical. The plants are best in full sun, in an open aspect. The soil should be well drained, but not necessarily rich. Remove finished flower stems, and cut back the plant to ground level as the foliage dies down in winter. Clumps are easily divided for propagation.

HELLEBORUS SPECIES & HYBRIDS
HELLEBORE

Jewel of the winter garden and the woodland floor, the hellebore is a plant of many wonderful talents. It thrives in shady conditions, has handsome foliage, and flowers from midwinter and early spring with blooms that last for months. While only a handful of species are commonly cultivated in the garden, including the green-flowered *Helleborus argutifolius*, *H. niger* with flowers of porcelain white, and *H. orientalis*, there are hybrids galore. Many of the modern hybrids derive from *H. orientalis*, and their flowers may be palest pink and white to cream and soft green, wine red, and dark burgundy, or intriguingly mottled.

GROWING NOTES
Most of the garden hellebores are evergreens that grow in small clumps to about 1–2 ft (30–60 cm) in height, and all have hand-shaped leaves. The plants prefer dappled sunlight or part

Also known as the winter rose, hellebores flower in winter and early spring—perfect companions at the feet of deciduous trees.

Hellebore flowers last for months in the garden, but also cut well for the vase; *Helleborus argutifolius* (opposite) is a species with green blooms.

shade and moist soil. Hellebores, with their winter-flowering habit, are perfect under deciduous trees.

There are cultivars of hellebores to suit climates from cold to temperate and warm; in their comfort zones, these perennials are long-lived and extremely easy to grow. Many of the modern hybrids also grow well in containers, particularly if kept shaded and moist. Older clumps can be divided, though they are agonizingly slow to re-establish, and plants are easily grown from seed and extremely conducive to hybridization. Seedlings will try the gardener's patience by taking years to bloom, but reward with the possibility of spectacularly unusual or uniquely beautiful flowers.

HOSTA SPECIES & CULTIVARS
HOSTA

The hostas, or plantain lilies, are the quintessential perennials for neutrally toned gardens that emphasize subtle color and striking form. There are hundreds of cultivars of these herbaceous ornamentals, deriving from species endemic to China, Korea, and mostly Japan; the majority are grown for their leaves that have variegations like works of horticultural art. Some of the species, and their cultivars, also have prominent spires of lily-like flowers to add to their charms, including *Hosta sieboldiana*, with blue-green leaves and white or lilac flowers, and *H. plantaginea*, which has delicately fragrant white blooms.

GROWING NOTES

All hostas are best in cool shady gardens, especially around sheltered water features or under trees. Some adapt to warmer gardens, given suitable microclimates. The plants need shade or dappled sun (this may also depend on leaf variegations), and will only tolerate stronger light in cold climates. The soil must be enriched before planting, and always moist. The clumps grow from fleshy rhizomes and may be divided (also a good way of rejuvenating plants every five years).

Most hostas are valued for exquisite leaves but some are grown for flowers, too; *Hosta plantaginea* (left) has fragrant white blooms.

HYDRANGEA SPECIES & CULTIVARS
HYDRANGEA

Many garden-grown hydrangeas are cultivars and varieties of the species *Hydrangea macrophylla,* including the lacecaps and most potted-color types.

For many years, the hydrangea has been subject to the whims of horticultural fashion, ever since the most well-known species, *Hydrangea macrophylla*, was introduced to 19th-century Europe from Japan (where it had long been in cultivation). In fact, hydrangeas never go out of style, either as cut flowers or in the garden.

Early in its cultivation days, the hydrangea was prized for its blue flowers (this occurs when some plants are grown in acidic soil that contains aluminum), but rightly we now value its many colored forms—from shocking pink to lilac to all the china blues and tints of white. Also popular is the lacecap (a variation of *H. macrophylla*) with its delicate floral style; dwarfed types (again of *H. macrophylla*) that grow no more than 2 ft (60 cm) in height; as well as the shrub-like species such as *H. quercifolia*, from North America, with its panicles of

creamy flower heads and lobed leaves. and the tall-growing *H. paniculata* with ivory-white blooms.Of course, gardeners are also notorious for impulse-buying of any potted-color hydrangeas; and though sometimes the flowers that catch our attention are artificially enhanced, we enjoy them anyway.

GROWING NOTES

Hydrangeas grow in most climates from tropical to cool, although very cold winters can damage them. The plants prefer the woodland conditions of their origins: dappled sunlight or morning sun only; rich, moist but well-drained soil; and protection from strong wind or hot sun. Cut back flowering stems as soon as they have finished, leaving any unflowered growth to produce next year's blooms. Prune hard to ground level every few years in winter to rejuvenate the plant. Hydrangeas are easily propagated from cuttings (the flowers being mostly sterile).

All hydrangeas are excellent cut flowers, and also maintain their form when dried. The blooms of the white-flowered species can't be artificially colored.

The flower heads of the perennial candytuft, *Iberis sempervirens*, produced in spring and early summer, are among the purest of garden whites.

IBERIS SEMPERVIRENS
CANDYTUFT

Most of the colorful forms of candytuft in gardens tend to be cultivated as annuals, having the habit of flowering themselves to exhaustion. The perennial species, *Iberis sempervirens*, is also prolific, with the intricate flower heads typical of the genus; however, it has greater endurance. From southern Europe, these evergreens are low-growing and often featured as edging or in rock gardens and flower borders. Their flower heads are among the purest of garden whites, enhanced by central yellow dots on each four-petaled bloom and the plant's dark green leaves. In the cultivar 'Snowflake,' the flower head is semi-spherical, giving it the appearance of a snowy dome.

GROWING NOTES

Iberis sempervirens suits a range of climates, from warm to cold, and is also tolerant of frost. The plants require full sun to slight shade, and well-drained, light soil. Remove flower heads as they finish, and lightly trim plants after blooming to keep them compact. Divide clumps for propagation, or take stem cuttings in summer.

LEUCANTHEMUM X SUPERBUM
SHASTA DAISY

The shasta daisy is one of the garden's wondrous beacons of light, and the genus name, *Leucanthemum*, literally means "white flower." Aptly, too, the meadow wildflower, *Leucanthemum vulgare*, is often known as the moon daisy for its night-time glow. In the garden, the perennial hybrid *Leucanthemum* x *superbum* and its many white cultivars (including those with double blooms, fringed ray petals, and all-white flower heads) are the most frequently grown—lighting up beds and borders, containers, courtyards, and balconies, either mixed and complementing other plants, or shimmering in masses on their own.

GROWING NOTES

All the common types of *Leucanthemum* (once classified as *Chrysanthemum maximum*) will thrive in climates from warm to cool. Shasta daisies are herbaceous, though in warmer climates they can be semi-evergreen. They prefer full sun, protection from strong wind, and well-drained soil. Regular watering during flowering in spring and summer will promote growth and blooms. To prolong the display, remove finished stems or cut flowers for the vase. Divide clumps for propagation, but only retain the younger sections with roots.

Shasta daisies brighten the garden, even glowing at night; these perennials are very easy to grow.

LILIUM SPECIES & CULTIVARS

LILY

Most garden-grown lilies flower between late spring and fall, with many types blooming around midsummer.

This amazing family, Liliaceae, is one of the largest groups of flowering plants, with innumerable individuals going by the name of lily. The 80 or so species in the genus *Lilium* are often called the true lilies, or liliums, and are distinguished by their trumpet-shaped blooms, tall leafy flowering stems and bulbs with fleshy scales. From this group alone, there are hundreds of cultivars, and liliums are grown all over the world, with specialist breeders, growers, and societies to honor them.

Among the most significant of liliums are some of the first plants in cultivation history—the white lily, *Lilium candidum*, a food crop that dates back well before the Christian Era but became associated with religious purity shortly after the Christian Era began; and the tiger lily, *L. tigrinum*, similarly ancient in China and Japan, where it had culinary purposes. Other liliums, now ornamentally grown or featured in hybridization, arrived in horticulture much later, during the plant-collecting heydays of the 18th and 19th centuries. Some of these include *L. auratum*, the golden-ray lily, from Japan; *L. martagon*, the Turk's cap lily, with recurved crimson petals

All lilies make outstanding cut flowers, but don't remove stems at ground level: cut them above the lowest sets of leaves instead. *Lilium longiflorum* is one of the best-loved, with numerous, large, and fragrant blooms.

and dark spots; *L. longiflorum*, the tall-grower with pure white blooms; and *L. regale*, which has petals that are lilac-pink on the outside and white within.

GROWING NOTES

Liliums have various growing requirements, depending on the cultivar's origin. Most are best in cool climates but several types also adapt to warmer gardens. The plants generally prefer light shade or dappled sunlight, but some tolerate more sun. The soil must be well drained and heavily enriched before planting. Protect from strong wind, and avoid overhead watering. While liliums are widely available, interested gardeners should seek specialist growers and societies.

POLYGONATUM MULTIFLORUM
SOLOMON'S SEAL

Appearing as if by woodland magic, this plant emerges seemingly from nowhere, an enchantment of leaves and flowers. Once highly regarded by early herbalists for its medicinal qualities, Solomon's seal grows from a knotty rhizome as a single stem, up to 3 ft (1 m) in length. Along this arching wand are two rows of large, finely veined and satin-smooth leaves that fan upwards and outwards like glaucous green wings. The flowers hang in a row from the stem's underside, tiny clusters of bone-china white bells, each one tipped with green.

The woodland charm of Solomon's seal flowers is magical, but its single-stemmed herbaceous habit also mingles well with other plants.

GROWING NOTES

Suitable only for cool climates, *Polygonatum multiflorum* prefers sheltered shady conditions, such as under deciduous trees or among shrubs, with humus-rich soil that is well drained but retains moisture. This herbaceous perennial is dormant in winter, reappearing in spring and flowering soon after. The rhizomes multiply to eventually form a clump; this can be divided but is slow to regain its full prowess.

PRATIA SPECIES
PRATIA

The elfin appeal of its tiny starry flowers and its ground-hugging mat of minute leaves has ensured the increasing popularity of pratia in all kinds of gardens. These evergreen perennials make their winsome appearances along woodland floors, in shady rockeries, beside paths, and between pavers, around water features, and in pots (either on their own or as an underplanting to shrubs and trees). Most have branching, creeping stems intricately interwoven in a tapestry that spreads along the garden floor and becomes dotted all over with flowers. In the commonly grown *Pratia pedunculata*, these are delicately shaded stars, in colors from pale to dark china blues to sparkling white. In some species, the flowers are followed by decorative mini purple fruits.

Pratias are diminutive ground covers with elfin leaves, flowers, and also fruit. *Pratia pedunculata* has starry blooms in hues of china blues to white.

GROWING NOTES
Most of the pratias are adaptable to climates from warm to cool. They will grow in sun or part shade, but require a constantly moist soil. These plants are ideal for damp conditions; they won't withstand drying out. They can be propagated from cuttings, but some species will spread by seed (unwanted plants are easy to remove).

ROMNEYA COULTERI
MATILIJA POPPY

The matilija poppy flowers from spring to summer, depending on the climate; most of the garden forms are hybrids or varieties, some with larger-than-usual blooms.

With diaphanous white petals and ruffled yellow centers, matilija poppies are easy to admire, but not always easy to grow. *Romneya coulteri*, the only species in cultivation, requires conditions similar to its native habitats in California of rugged rocky country and dry riverbeds; the climate has hot, dry summers and rainy winters, and the soil is sandy or gravelly, and very well drained. Also known as the Californian tree poppy, this evergreen perennial, in ideal conditions, can grow to more than 6 ft (2 m) in height and spread via suckers into a dramatic shrub of deeply divided blue-green leaves, but in gardens it is usually more tame.

GROWING NOTES

With appropriate conditions, matilija poppies will grow in climates from cool to warm. The plants also need full sun all day. They don't like clay soils, high humidity, or summer rain. Remove flowers as they finish and, because the plants flower on new growth, cut back foliage to ground level in winter. Propagate from root cuttings or suckers.

THYMUS SPECIES & HYBRIDS

THYME

The botanical world of thyme is a complex place. There are more than 300 species in *Thymus*, endemic across Europe to Asia, and the differences between some of them are minute, even microscopic. Ornamentally, thymes are usually divided into two groups based on growth habit: shrubby types, such as the common thyme (*Thymus vulgaris*), and ground-covering forms, like wild thyme (*T. serpyllum*). Much favored in gardens as well is *T.* x *citriodorus*, the lemon thyme, which has a distinct scent and flavor. Also among the many hybrids or cultivars of thyme are plants with colorful leaves, from golden-yellow to variegated to silvery white.

GROWING NOTES

Thyme will grow in most climates from cool to subtropical, but it does prefer low humidity. The plants need full sun all day and very well drained soil, though not rich. Collections of thyme are easily amassed through divisions or cuttings (such gardeners are called "thymophiles"), and when various types are planted together and allowed to mingle, *au naturel*, the effect can be sensational.

In the garden, thyme has myriad uses: in pots, rockeries, edging, as ground cover, in lawns, or mass planted for a sensational tapestry.

TRILLIUM SPECIES

TRILLIUM

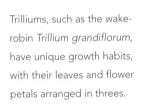

Curious perennials of woodland places, trilliums (though related to lilies) have distinct growth habits of three-leaved whorls and three-petaled flowers. Most of the species are native to North America and go by such folksy names as the wake-robin (*Trillium grandiflorum*), the painted wood-lily (*T. undulatum*), toadshade (*T. sessile*), and birthroot or stinking Benjamin (*T. erectum*). The wake-robin is the most commonly seen in gardens, often as a lush ground cover or under trees, with its broad, fanned leaves (in threes, of course) and tri-petaled white flowers that mature to deep pink. Its cultivars include 'Roseum,' which has all-pink blooms.

Trilliums, such as the wake-robin *Trillium grandiflorum*, have unique growth habits, with their leaves and flower petals arranged in threes.

GROWING NOTES

All trilliums prefer cool to cold conditions, though they will adapt to suitable microclimates in warmer gardens (such as in cool moist mountainous areas). The plants are naturally suited to woodland styles, and enjoy the dappled sun and rich soils of these environments. Though it may be interesting to grow them from seed (the seedlings being variable), these take many years to flower; division of established plants is easier.

In the species
Zantedeschia aethiopica
(above), the flowers have
pure white spathes.
'Green Goddess' (right)
is a cultivar.

ZANTEDESCHIA AETHIOPICA
ARUM LILY

The arum lily is an architectural wonder in the world of flowering plants. It has a central column of minuscule yellow flowers, the spadix, surrounded by a swirling spathe like a gown of white satin. Underground it is anchored and fed by a sturdy rhizome. The leaves, elegantly tapered and fleshy green, may also be splashed with silvery white, a perfect complement to the plant's natural setting, the watery habitats of South Africa.

So well-designed is *Zantedeschia aethiopica* that it can become a noxious weed where conditions suit, such as in warm temperate, especially close to waterways. Even when grown in large pots, which the plants fill with ease, they can become a nuisance—they self-seed freely and even the smallest slither of rhizome can reshoot. However, where caution is required, the arum's colorful relatives, commonly known as calla lilies (see page 204), are usually much more benign.

GROWING NOTES

Not surprisingly arum lilies thrive in a wide variety of climates from very cold to tropical. Though the plants prefer a moist soil, and even wet conditions, they aren't fussy and the dormant rhizomes can also be quite resistant to drought. The plants grow and flower in sun or shade, but look and do their best in dappled light. They are easily (often too easily) propagated from seed or by divisions of rhizomes. The plants may bloom from late winter through spring and sometimes into early summer. Both the flowers and the leaves are very long-lasting in arrangements, and even a single stem makes a most elegant cut flower.

Arum lilies form lush clumps of verdant leaf, crowned in spring and summer by stems of lightly fragrant flowers.

ZEPHYRANTHES CANDIDA
RAIN LILY

The flowers of rain lilies appear throughout summer and sometimes also fall, but especially after downpours. *Zephyranthes candida* is the most common species.

The rain lily is also called the storm lily for its habit of flowering profusely after downpours, although its botanical name, *Zephyranthes*, means "flower of the West Wind." Originating from tropical America and the West Indies, these bulbous perennials are favored in warm-climate gardens both for their funnel-shaped flowers and their evergreen reed-like leaves. The plants form thick but neat tufts that can be used in expansive grass-like edgings, but are also effective as small accent clumps, as underplanting, or in pots. The most widely grown species, *Zephyranthes candida,* has white flowers in late summer or fall, but increasingly popular is *Z. grandiflora*, with strappier-shaped leaves and pale pink summer flowers.

GROWING NOTES

Rain lilies prefer warm to hot or tropical conditions but also grow in suitable microclimates in cooler areas. Some types behave herbaceously (with the foliage dying down) during cold winters or drought. The plants require dappled sunlight or morning sun only, and well-drained soil. Clumps can be divided for propagation, but a crowd of bulbs produces better displays of leaf and flower.

iris

The iris is the flower of the rainbow, by nature and by name. Its botanical title, *Iris*, honors the rainbow goddess of Greek mythology, and it is one of few plants that can claim all the flower colors. Irises were among the first plants in cultivation, although ancient types were subtly toned. Now, no flower can compare.

Legend attests that the iris was one of the first plants in cultivation—depictions of irises have been found on Cretan frescoes and Egyptian temples which are thousands of years old. *Iris germanica*, the original bearded iris, has been cultivated for many centuries, not only for its scented and beautiful flowers but also for the fragrant roots of the cultivar 'Florentina,' the source of orris, a wonder-herb of medieval days and still widely used today. Some say that *I. germanica* was the inspiration for the fleur-de-lis, while others say it was the flag iris, *I. pseudoacorus*—whatever the species, it was definitely an iris that was adopted as that emblem of the French royalty, somewhere around the mid-1100s CE.

In the East, too, where many irises originate, they were highly valued. *Iris laevigata* features in some of the oldest known Japanese poetry, as well as its art, but *I. ensata* (syn. *I. kaempferi*) also has a very long history. The Japanese irises that we know now are hybrids—recognized mostly by their flattish flowers, some with petals wavy or frilled—and their exact origins are somewhat obscure, having been cultivated for centuries in China and Japan before they were introduced to Europe and elsewhere.

The Louisiana irises (opposite), as well as the Japanese and Siberian types, thrive in damp soil beside water features and ponds. Previous page: The flag iris, *Iris pseudoacorus*, is a water-lover too.

Irises flower in spring and early summer. With their extensive color range and tidy habits, they mix well in borders with other flowers, such as these poppies.

The iris family (Iridaceae) is one of the most numerous of flowering plants, and found naturally in many parts of the world. Of these, only about 200 species are true irises, from the genus *Iris*: these have the characteristic flower with three falls (the pendent petals), three standards (usually the upward-sweeping ones), and a three-branched style.

There are now so many irises that the genus has split. The iris group best known as perennials in the garden are those that grow from rhizomes (the Dutch iris, also popular, grows from a bulb). These rhizomatous irises, as they are horticulturally known, are also classified into two broad groups: the bearded types, distinguished by the colored hairs at the center of each fall, are based on *I. germanica*; and the beardless, which includes the Japanese, Louisiana, and Siberian forms.

All these rhizomatous irises, apart from displaying an infinite range of flower colors, have very different growing requirements—which means there are irises for almost any kind of garden. The bearded irises will grow in most warm to cool climates, but the climatic needs of the beardless group varies: Louisiana irises, hybrids of North American species, prefer to grow where the summers are hot, while Japanese and Siberian irises are best in gardens that are cool to cold.

The rhizomatous irises include the flag cultivars (top left); the bearded irises derived from *Iris germanica* (top and bottom right); and the many Japanese hybrids (bottom left).

GROWING NOTES

All the rhizomatous irises generally have strap-shaped leaves and grow in fanned basal clumps that are attractive even out of flower. The plants prefer full sun and some shelter from strong wind. For best growth, the soil should always be enriched with aged organic matter before planting, but beware of some exact requirements. Bearded irises prefer well drained, slightly limey soil. The beardless types all require moist soil conditions, and they may be grown in marginal areas around water features such as ponds (some will even grow in water); but of these the Japanese irises must have their soil acidic. All irises enjoy generous watering during the growing season and while in flower. Remove flower stems as they finish, and also any foliage that has aged and dried. Clumps of irises can be divided for propagation, but cut off the leaves into a short fan to help the plants recover.

Discerning garden centers will proffer some very good varieties of the major types, but if you find yourself wanting more, visit an iris show, society, or specialist nursery and get the full rainbow spectacular.

Irises are the most colorful blooms in cultivation, with flowers from indigo to gold, as well as diaphanous white and infinite shades of blue, purple, yellow, and pink.

PROPAGATION
NOTES

Plant propagation is a great skill that all gardeners can learn. Here are a few tips in relation to flowering perennials.

SEEDS

Many species of perennials will produce seeds from which new plants can be grown. However, most hybrids and cultivars don't produce viable seeds—even if they do set seed, the resulting seedlings often don't come "true," which means they may differ from the parent or revert to an original form without the selected traits. Some perennials flower quickly from seedlings, but many don't and you may have to wait a few years or agonizingly longer.

CUTTINGS

Cuttings are quick and easy means of propagation, requiring only small sections of healthy stem. Cuttings are usually about 2–8 in (5–20 cm) long, depending on the plant's habit. There are three main types: softwood or tip, semi-hardwood, and hardwood. Softwood or tip cuttings are usually taken from new, unflowered shoots in the growing season; trim the stem just below a node and remove all but the top few leaves. Semi-hardwood cuttings are similar but taken later, using more mature stems that are green at the tip but starting to turn woody at the base. Hardwood cuttings are normally taken during winter, while plants are dormant; these are bare stems without any leaves. Cuttings should be planted into a well-drained, light potting medium (such as coarse sand and compost, or a propagation mix) that is kept constantly moist. Misting or placing the cuttings in a humid environment will help them recover, but be careful of overwatering: cuttings are just as easily lost through rotting as by drying out.

DIVISIONS AND ROOT CUTTINGS

Many perennials grow in clumps or via spreading stems and these plants are easily propagated. To divide a clump, dig the whole plant carefully out of the ground and then separate the clump into sections, each with a strong batch of roots. Trim any broken roots and also reduce foliage before replanting; then water regularly to establish. Perennials that grow from tubers or rhizomes can also be propagated by dividing in this way. For trailing perennials or ground covers, dig up a section or stem with roots, separate it from the parent, and replant the division.

Similarly, some perennials can also be propagated from root cuttings. These are small sections of roots, about ¼ in (5 mm) thick, removed from the main root clump. The root cutting should be carefully washed of soil, then planted either vertically (if necessary, mark the cutting when taking it so you know which way is "up") or horizontally; containers of well-drained potting medium are ideal. As with all cuttings, keep the soil moist but do not overwater.

GLOSSARY

ACID SOIL: soil that has a pH of less than 7.

ALKALINE SOIL: soil that has a pH of greater than 7.

ANNUAL: a plant that has a natural lifecycle of one season, usually within a year.

AXIL: the part of the plant where the leaf joins the stem.

BIENNIAL: a plant that has a natural lifecycle of two years.

BRACT: a modified leaf attached to a flower or cluster of flowers; sometimes brightly colored.

CALYX: the outer part of a flower; it consists of sepals and is sometimes brightly colored or decorative.

COMPOUND LEAF: any leaf that is made up of two or more leaflets.

CORM: an underground part of the plant used for food storage, and from which roots and leaves emerge.

COROLLA: the part of a flower that is formed by the petals.

CROWN: the plant part where the stems meet the soil; new shoots grow from the top, with roots from the bottom.

CULTIVAR: a distinct form of plant that has different features from the species; usually a result of selected breeding or cultivation.

CUTTING: a section of leaf, stem, or root that is separated from a plant in order to reproduce it.

DEAD-HEADING: the removal of finished flowers in order to prevent seeds from forming, and to encourage the production of new blooms.

DECIDUOUS PLANT: a plant that loses its leaves annually as part of its natural lifecycle.

DIVISION: a method of propagation by dividing a plant clump into smaller sections.

DOUBLE FLOWER: a flower that has more petals than the usual number in the species.

FAMILY: a group of related plants; includes genera and species.

FLORET: a single flower in a composite arrangement or head of many flowers.

GENUS: closely related plants, within a family, that share many characteristics; includes species.

HABIT: the plant's usual form, appearance, and way of growing.

HYBRID: a plant which is the result of crossing different genera, species, or cultivars.

INFLORESCENCE: a flowering stem of more than one flower.

NODE: the part of a stem from which the leaf or bud grows.

PANICLE: a branched raceme.

PEDICEL: the stalk of an individual flower.

RACEME: an unbranched flowering stem of stalked flowers, with the youngest at the top.

RHIZOME: a plant part used for food storage; may be underground or above ground; is usually horizontal.

SEPAL: a petal-like structure that forms part of the calyx.

SPECIES: very closely related plants, within a genus; the basic unit of classification.

TUBER: an underground part of the plant used for food storage, derived from a root or stem.

UMBEL: a flat or rounded inflorescence with the flower stems arising from one point.

VARIETY: a particular type of a plant that has different features to the species but occurs naturally.

PHOTO CREDITS

DELL ADAM: 134 bottom, 135, 225.

BAY PICTURE LIBRARY: back cover top R, 45, 53, 54, 58 top R, 70, 75, 84, 87 top, 90, 97, 99 bottom, 124–5, 137, 143, 149, 164, 172 top, 174, 178, 180, 187, 194, 229, 232, 240, 244, 254, 255, 268, 272, 288, 292, 322 bottom, 361, 362–3, 367, 413, 414, 420, 423, 424, 428, 455, 458, 464.

JOE FILSHIE: back cover bottom R, 30–1, 46, 48–9, 61 bottom, 67, 69, 71, 95, 99 top, 115, 116 bottom L, 136, 139, 144–5, 146, 151, 162–3, 172 bottom, 173, 175, 182, 204, 220, 228, 234, 242, 246, 251 bottom R, 252 top, 260, 263, 290, 298 (bottom L and R), 302 bottom L, 320–1, 339, 344, 348–9, 350–1, 355, 356–7, 358–9, 366, 369, 371, 372 top, 379, 380, 418, 426, 433, 439, 440 bottom, 443 top, 444 top, 446, 447 bottom, 449, 452, 454, 456–7, 467, 469, 473, 476–7, 478 (top R, bottom L and R).

ANDRÉ MARTIN: 26.

MURDOCH BOOKS PHOTO LIBRARY: 41, 56, 58 (top L and bottom L), 106, 236, 239, 293, 335, 471.

LORNA ROSE: back cover (top L and bottom R), 6–7, 8, 11, 14–15, 16, 22–3, 32–3, 34–5, 36–7, 38–9, 40, 42–3, 47, 50–1, 52, 55, 57, 59, 60, 61 top, 62–63, 65, 66, 68, 72–3, 74, 76, 78–9, 81, 82–3, 85, 86, 87 bottom, 88–9, 91, 92–93, 94, 98, 100–1, 102–3, 104–5, 107, 109, 110–11, 112–13, 116 (top L and R, bottom R), 118–19, 120, 123, 126–7, 128–9, 130–1, 132–3, 140–1, 142, 147, 150, 152–3, 154–5, 156–7, 158–9, 160–1, 165, 166–7, 170–1, 176–7, 179, 183, 184, 185 bottom, 186, 188–9, 190–1, 192–3, 196–7, 198–9, 200–1, 203,

205, 206–7, 208–9, 210, 212–13, 214–15, 217, 218–19, 221, 222, 224, 226, 231, 233, 235, 237, 238, 241, 243, 252 bottom, 253, 256, 258–9, 262, 265, 266–7, 269, 271, 273, 274–5, 276–7, 279, 280–1, 282, 284–5, 287, 289, 294–5, 298 (top L and R), 300–1, 302 (top L and bottom R), 305, 306–7, 308–9, 310–11, 312–13, 314–15, 316–17, 318–19, 322 top, 323, 324, 326–7, 328–9, 330–1, 332, 334, 336–7, 338, 340–341, 342–3, 346–7, 352–3, 354, 364–5, 368, 370, 373, 374–5, 376–7, 381, 382–3, 384, 386–7, 388–9, 390–1, 394–5, 396–7, 398–9, 400–1, 402–3, 404–5, 406–7, 408–9, 410, 415, 417, 419, 422, 425, 429, 430–1, 432 top L, 434–5, 437, 440 top, 441, 442, 448, 450–1, 453, 460–1, 462–3, 465, 466, 468, 470, 474 (top L and bottom L), 478 top L, 481.

SUE STUBBS: front cover, 2, 4, 12, 19, 20, 25, 29, 64, 134 top, 185 top, 211, 230, 249, 250, 251 top L, 283, 333, 372 bottom, 392–3, 416, 436, 443 bottom, 444 bottom, 445, 474 (top R and bottom R), 482–3, 484, 487, 489, 490, 493, 494.

PAT TAYLOR: 432 top R.

JAMES YOUNG: 261, 264.

THE PUBLISHER WOULD LIKE TO ACKNOWLEDGE PHOTOGRAPHY IN THE FOLLOWING GARDENS: Al-ru farm, Australia; Amberley, New Zealand; Ayrlies, New Zealand; Bay Cottage, Australia; Briar Rose Cottage, New Zealand; Bringalbit, Australia; Buskers End, Australia; Convent Gallery, Australia; Curry Flat, Australia; Dunedin, Australia; Gethsemane Gardens, New Zealand; Hedgerow Roses, Australia; Heronswood, Australia; Kevin Kilsby Ceramics, New Zealand; Kooringal, Australia; Lyddington, New Zealand; Ngodevwa, New Zealand; P&S Lawrence, New Zealand; Red Cow Farm, Australia; Saumarez Homestead, Australia; Tregamere, New Zealand; Woodleigh Farm, New Zealand.

INDEX

cinquefoil, 108–9
Cistus, 52–3
Clivia miniata, 162–3
columbine, 144–7
Convallaria majalis, 418–19
Convolvulus mauritanicus, 228–9
  C. sabatius, 228
Coreopsis, 164
Corydalis cashmeriana, 230
  C. lutea, 230
cowslip, 374
cranesbill, 248
Crassula arborescens, 420
  C. multicava, 420–1
cut-leaf daisy, 336–7
Cyclamen hederifolium, 55
  C. persicum, 55
Cymbidium, 422–5
Cynara cardunculus, 232–3

dahlia, 56–9
daisy bush, 322
daylily, 182–5
dead-nettle, 352–3
Delphinium, 234–7
Dianthus caryophyllus, 343
  D. deltoides, 344
  D. plumarius, 343–5
desert candles, 426–7
Diascia cordata, 347
  D. rigescens, 347
Dicentra spectabilis, 60–1
Dichorisandra thyrsiflora, 238–9
Dierama pulcherrimum, 62–3
Dietes bicolor, 166–7
  D. grandiflora, 166

Digitalis purpurea, 348–51
dyer's chamomile, 142–3

Easter daisy, 40–3
Echinacea purpurea, 64–5
Echinops bannaticus, 241
  E. ritro, 241
  E. sphaerocephalus, 241
Echium candicans, 242–3
  E. fastuosum, 242–3
Egyptian star cluster, 105
Eremurus himalaicus, 427
  E. olgae, 427
  E. robustus, 427
Erigeron aureus, 428
  E. karvinskianus, 428–9
Eryngium maritimum, 431
  E. planum, 431
  E. variifolium, 431
Euphorbia characias subsp.
    wulfenii, 432–5
  E. marginata, 432
  E. pulcherrima, 432
  E. robbiae, 435
Euryops pectinatus, 168–9
evening primrose, 364–5

fairy fishing rods, 62–3
fan flower, 284–5
Felicia amelloides, 244–5
flame of the woods, 79
flaming Katy, 80–3
fleabane, 428–9
foxglove, 348–51
foxtail lily, 426–7
fuchsia, 66–9

Fuchsia fulgens, 66
  F. magellanica, 66

Gaillardia aristata, 170
  G. x grandiflora, 170
Gaura lindheimeri, 436–7
Gazania x *hybrida*, 124–5,
    172–5
  G. rigens, 175
Gentiana acaulis, 246–7
Geraldton waxflower, 340–1
geranium, 248–51
Geranium x *cantabrigiense*
    'Biokovo', 250–1
  G. x *magnificum*, 248–9
Gerbera jamesonii, 70
Geum, 72–3
  G. x *borisii*, 73
  G. rivale, 73
ginger lily, 176–7
globe thistle, 240–1
gold dust, 150–1
golden-ray lily, 452
goldenrod, 202–3
golden tuft, 150–1
golden wand lily, 152–3

harebell, 223, 224
Hedychium coccineum, 177
  H. coronarium, 177
  H. gardnerianum, 176–7
Helenium autumnale, 178–9
Helianthemum nummularium,
    74–5
Heliopsis helianthoides, 180–1
heliotrope, 252–3

Michaelmas daisy, 40–1
milfoil, 316–19
milkweed, 432
Monarda didyma, 92–3
moon daisy, 451
Moroccan glory bind, 228–9
moutan, 368
musk mallow, 363

Nepeta cataria, 264
  N. x faassenii, 264–5

obedient plant, 106–7
Oenothera acaulis, 364
  O. biennis, 364
  O. speciosa, 364–5
  O. tetragona, 364
orchid, 422–5
oriental poppy, 94–5
Osteospermum barberae, 367
  O. ecklonis, 367
Oswego tea, 92–3
oyster plant, 402–3

Paeonia lactiflora, 30–1, 368
  P. suffruticosa, 368
painted wood-lily, 465
Papaver orientale, 94–5
paper daisy, 338–9
pasque flower, 276–7
pelargonium, 26, 96–9
Pelargonium x domesticum, 96
  P. x hortorum, 96–7
  P. peltatum, 99
Penstemon, 100–3
Pentas lanceolata, 104–5
peony, 368–71

perennials
  bare-rooted, 18, 21
  definition of, 10
  general care of, 21, 24
  planting, 18, 21
  pruning, 24
  propagation of, 27, 485–6
  types of, 10, 13
periwinkle, 290–1, 415
Peruvian lily, 136–9
Phlomis fruticosa, 192–3
Phlox paniculata, 372–3
  P. subulata, 372
Physostegia virginiana, 106–7
pickerel rush, 272–3
pin-cushion flower, 255
pinks, 343–5
Platycodon grandiflorus, 266–7
Plectranthus australis, 268
  P. saccatus, 268–9
poinsettia, 432
Polemonium caeruleum, 270–1
Polygonatum multiflorum, 456–7
Pontederia cordata, 272–3
Potentilla, 108–9
Pratia, 458–9
  P. pedunculata, 458–9
pride of Madeira, 242–3
primrose, 374–7
Primula denticulata, 374
  P. malacoides, 377
  P. obconica, 376–7
  P. x polyantha, 377
  P. sieboldii, 377
  P. veris, 374
  P. vulgaris, 374, 377
Pulmonaria, 274–5

Pulsatilla vulgaris, 276–7
purple coneflower 64–5, 392–3
purple loosestrife, 360

rain lily, 470–1
Ranunculus acris, 194–5
red hot poker, 188–91
red valerian, 50–1
Rehmannia elata, 378–9
Rhodohypoxis baurii, 380–1
rock cress, 410–11
rock rose, 52–3, 74
Romneya coulteri, 460–1
Rosa, 114–23
  R. chinensis, 116
  R. x damascena, 117
rose, 114–23
rose campion, 91
rose grass, 380–1
rose of Sharon, 187
rosemary, 278–9
Rosmarinus officinalis, 278–9
Rudbeckia laciniata, 129, 196–7
Russell lupins, 356–9

sage, 280–3
  culinary, 281
  mealy cup, 282
  Mexican, 281
salvia, 280–3
Salvia farinacea, 280–2
  S. leucantha, 281
  S. officinalis, 281
  S. patens, 283
  S. splendens, 281
sandwort, 412–13
satin flower, 384–5

Murdoch Books® Australia
GPO Box 2001
Sydney NSW 1045
Phone: + 61 (0) 2 4352 7000
Fax: + 61 (0) 2 4352 7026

Murdoch Books UK Limited
Ferry House, 51–57 Lacy Road
Putney, London SW15 1PR
Phone: + 44 (0) 20 8355 1480
Fax: + 44 (0) 20 83551499

Published in 2003 by Bay Books, an imprint of Murdoch Magazines Pty Ltd.

ISBN 1 74045 325 5

Printed by Midas Printing (Asia) Ltd
PRINTED IN CHINA

Text: Susin Leong
Design: Tracy Loughlin
Design Concept: Marylouise Brammer
Creative Director: Marylouise Brammer
Editorial Director: Diana Hill
Production: Janis Barbi

Chief Executive: Juliet Rogers
Publisher: Kay Scarlett